FLAMIN' ECK

MEMOIRS OF A YORKSHIRE FIREFIGHTER

MARK COOKE

To my wife Janine, without whose help and input this book would have never made it to print. All my love Mark.

First published in Great Britain in 2024

Copyright © Mark Cooke

The moral right of the author has been asserted.

All rights reserved.

No part of this publication may be reproduced, stored in a retrieval system, or transmitted, in any form or by any means, without the prior permission in writing of the publisher, nor be otherwise circulated in any form of binding or cover other than that in which it is published and without a similar condition including this condition being imposed on the subsequent purchaser.

Editing, design, typesetting and publishing by UK Book Publishing.

www.ukbookpublishing.com

ISBN: 978-1-917329-47-7

It was 3.00am on a cold winter's night. Silence was the order of this time of day. Darkness and the stillness of the middle of the night. Then the lights burst on at the same time as the sudden jolting bang of the alerter coming into life with its pulsating, repetitive "beep, beep, beep, beep".

Although my bed was the furthest away from the dormitory door, at the end of a long row of ten beds lining up, side by side, I would be the first dressed and running down the dormitory. Others as I passed them were scrambling to pull up trousers etc in the dash to get dressed. At the end of the dorm, I pulled a little brass handle, and two wooden doors flipped open, revealing a pole from the floor above us and one directly in front of me down to the ground floor. I grabbed hold and as I slid down, over the station tannoy, a voice shouted.

"Persons reported?" came the voice of my Station Officer who slept on the ground floor and had obviously arrived at the printer first which had whirred all the details of the incident out.

"Persons reported" was the command that all firefighters the world over would respond to with the same reaction.

A massive injection of adrenaline to their system. It meant there was a fire with people trapped inside.

Running into the engine house, the three appliances lined up, I ran along pulling on three large ropes with a big knot on each end. This released the three double doors that were on springs, each slamming back, folding with a loud clank, opening the warm engine house to the cold dark world outside.

I was in the back of the water ladder that night, which was the first pump of the three lined up and the one the Station Officer, who was in charge, rode on. The mad scramble of putting on fire kit whilst the starting of vehicle engines occurred. I climbed into the rear of the appliance, finishing fastening my tunic at the same time. A head peered round from the front of the cab, my Station Officer shouting "Two BAs!" The breathing apparatus sets were stored in racks behind us on the seats so we could pull them on as we travelled. I could hear the sound of the vehicle radio starting up and the operator at control repeating our call sign.

"Go ahead, pass your message!" our Station Officer replied.

"We are receiving numerous calls to this incident" came the voice of the control operator. "Calls state that the house is well alight with several people trapped." The operator paused. "'Callsign', did you receive?"

"Received, and understood," replied the boss, again, turning to us as we were now pulling out of the engine house. "Hear that, lads? It's a goer!"

So, lights flashing and reflecting in the dark, we sped off. The driver who had picked up the printed message shouted out the address. It was an area we all knew so thankfully there wasn't a scramble looking at maps for directions.

We sped along the roads which were clear at that time of the night. My head whizzing with several checklists of gear, procedures, equipment needed and my heart pounding with adrenaline at the thought of what we would find on arrival.

This was my first real going fire since I had been stationed here several weeks ago and my first ever "Persons reported".

As we got nearer, we could see a plume of billowing smoke rising in the clear sky. This was an area of old late nineteenth/early twentieth century, terraced houses, street after street. These streets housed a large Asian Community of Pakistani and Bangladeshi origin. Families going back two or three generations who had come to work in the mills and factories in the town.

We turned around the corner onto the street; flames were visibly pouring from the downstairs window of the house and large amounts of smoke billowed upwards on the outside of the house.

"Start-up, lads," the Station Officer said, peering round at us again.

A large amount of people was now standing in the street, some waving their arms frantically in the air. As we came to a stop and climbed out of the cab, we were bombarded with numerous people running up to us, shouting and gesticulating furiously. One woman, head in her hands, screeching in Punjabi then broken English, "My son and children, children in house!"

We didn't know that prior to this point several members of the household had already jumped out of the bathroom at the rear of the house onto an outhouse and into the backyard, helped by neighbours.

The scene was chaotic, the sounds of people shouting and screaming, fire crackling and banging, and the revving of the fire engine as the driver got the pumps into gear and ready to go! My partner and I started pulling off the hose reel from the fire engine, running it in loops on the floor so we could pull it into the house.

"Knock that fire down and get upstairs," the Station Officer shouted at us.

We fired our jet through the window, knocking the flames back as quickly as we could. Even more steam and smoke poured back out of the window, hitting the cold night air and billowing into the sky. Another team arrived with a larger length of hose, firing their jet into the window.

"Get inside and upstairs," shouted the boss. "There are people still inside."

If a fire is a 'persons reported' then automatically three fire appliances are despatched; two from our station were there and another from the next nearest station would be alerted and sent. The Ambulance service and Police would also be immediately informed.

The two Breathing Apparatus wearers from the other appliance had also started up and were stood behind us as we entered. Me and my partner Mick crouched down as we entered the front of the house. Even though we were crouched down, the heat hit us in the face, especially our ears, or as my Subo at training school had called them 'your thermometers'. This room was clearly where the seat of the fire was. As the jet that the other crew fired through the window hit the heat, gusts of steam caused us to crouch even further to the ground to try and escape the heat. I had turned my jet to a spray of about 45° with the hose reel gun held in my hands. We had seen from outside that there was an attic with a dormer window all blackened with smoke as were the other first floor windows at the front. Crouched down, we could see fairly reasonably in this room so we made our way to the bottom of the stairs, the other pair assisting us, pulling the hose in behind us so that we could progress quickly. We could just see the bottom couple of steps, but beyond this it was just thick black smoke.

"Ok, Mick." I turned and spoke to my partner. "Let's get up to the top floor to search, tell the other crew to feed the hose reel up behind us and get them to search the first floor," I shouted through my breathing mask.

"Ok," he replied. As I pulled the hose reel up the stairs in the pitch darkness, I could hear him relaying the message to the other team. It was hot! The heat had built up during the fire downstairs and, as it does, had gone up the stairs, filling it with thick hot darkness. It had only taken a minute or two to get to this point. On we went in the heat and darkness, along the landing, feeling the walls with our hands, sweeping the floor with our feet, to try and get some sense of direction.

There wasn't any fire upstairs that we could visibly see, no glowing through the smoke, just the thick, black, hot darkness. I reached a door, pulled my glove back, felt the door and handle with the back of my hand. It didn't feel any hotter than the surrounding area, so I pulled it slowly open. The smoke had found its way through the old ill-fitting door; it was not too thick at that moment but there was still no visibility. The area was full of the sounds of clattering and banging of the other crew and Mick pulling the hose reel up the stairs behind me. I felt behind the door with my foot and could feel that it was the stairs going up to the attic.

"I've found the stairs," I shouted at Mick.

"Right," he replied.

"We're going upstairs to check the attic," I shouted as loudly as I could so the other crew could hear.

Dragging more hose reel up the stairs, we proceeded. A doorway was open at the top of the stairs so again in the darkness we felt our way in. I went on the right wall and Mick went left along that wall, both of us feeling with our hands and feet for any signs of casualties. We were taught at training school there is nothing you don't check in or under in a fire situation. People, and in particular children, do the strangest things in panic in a fire situation. Children especially want the situation to go away and in their little minds if you can't see it, it's not there. This means they are likely to climb into cupboards, wardrobes, under beds etc, to make it go away.

A shout came across the room from Mick. "I've found a bloody cot."

"What?" I replied, with the Darth Vader sound of breathing. Communicating in breathing apparatus was difficult at the best of times, but with both of our breathing rates increased, it was even more difficult.

"A cot," he shouted again. "I can't feel anything in it, it's empty!" he continued.

At that point my foot hit what at first felt like a pile of soft rags. I bent down and could tell it was a torso, my hands continued feeling upwards then I felt its head. "I've found one," I shouted at Mick. "He's here on the floor by the bed."

The casualty was a male and he felt fairly slim. I reached under his arms as his head just flopped to one side. He was clearly unconscious.

Mick came over and felt in the darkness for the casualty's legs. "I've got his legs," he said to me. "Have you got hold of him?" he asked. In the heat the casualty had actually become so hot and sweaty he just felt like he was covered in grease. As I tried to lift him around his chest his arms just flopped together above his head sliding through my arms and flopping back on the floor, his pyjama top now scrunched up and wrapped around his head and shoulders. In frustration I grabbed him again, this time looping my arms through and around; grabbing his wrists I lifted him off the floor. This did the trick.

"Ok, I've got him," I shouted.

"I'll take the lead," Mick said.

We headed back through the still-thick smoke, retracing our steps using the picture we had built up in our minds of the room in the last few minutes. Mick continued leading me and instructing me as to what was coming ahead. We got back to the first floor and could hear the other team in the darkness and shouted that we had found a casualty. On the second flight of stairs down to the ground floor the hold I had on the casualty slipped again with the sweat and oiliness of the poor chap's skin and I dropped him. The trouble was Mick didn't realise, and legs in hand continued down the stairs. The poor gentleman on his back, head clattering step by step, bang, bang, bang as he went.

"I've lost hold," I shouted frantically at Mick.

"I've just gathered," he replied, realising the poor gentleman's speedy progress down the stairs. I grabbed hold of him yet again and we sped out of the building, casualty in hand, as fast as we could. On exiting the building, a stretcher with two ambulance personnel stood by it, beckoning us to put him on it.

Outside was a scene of flashing blue lights of Fire, Police and Ambulances. Neighbours, family and friends frantically wanting to know what was going on and was our gentleman Ok? We put him onto the stretcher and quickly regained as much dignity as we could for him by re arranging his clothing.

The casualty's breathing and circulation were quickly assessed, and both were found to be very poor. He was quickly put onto oxygen and moved straight into the ambulance.

The Station Officer came over to us and asked for an update and had we searched all of the attic?

"Not all," we both replied.

"How much air have you got?" he asked us. We both looked at our gauges and they were both nearing our whistle time. This meant that we hadn't enough air to continue.

"Ok, shut down both of you, I'll get another crew to check." He shouted over at two more firefighters with breathing apparatus who had not started up but were ready, and told them to go straight up to the attic and search.

"Well done, lads," he said to us both.

We walked across and back to our appliance both with streams of steam rising off us in the cold night. Soon all people were accounted for; a couple of other people had also suffered from smoke inhalation and minor injuries from escaping out of the rear windows. Thankfully, all children and one baby had all been rescued safely. The fire scene quietened down, those needing more than basic first aid taken to hospital. We would be there for several hours more after the initial pandemonium as is the case with any fire like this. Time spent venting, removing still smouldering possessions. Setting up lighting so that Fire Investigation could see and establish a possible cause. Removing floorboards, ceiling plaster to check that there was no smouldering fire that had not been extinguished.

The Station Officer I had at that time though had the trait of leaving the incident at the earliest opportunity. He would put it in the hands of either the Sub Officer or Leading Fireman, whoever was next in charge. So came the shout: "Right, water ladder crew, get our gear back on board, we're off!"

Arriving back at the station all the gear which had been used had to be cleaned or replaced straight away, so we were fully kitted up ready to go again.

The tannoy went; "Pot of fire tea ready" came the instruction. After any working job at the first opportunity a pot of strong tea would be made, plonked on the mess table surrounded by mugs, milk and sugar at the ready. This would be a time to go through what we had done, an unofficial debrief.

The Station Officer came into the mess room where we were all sat down, cups in hands. "I've just been in contact with A &

E, the guy has suffered severe smoke inhalation although not going into any details he is in Intensive Care, but he is breathing normally on his own and is expected to make a full recovery."

Apparently, he had gone back up to the attic thinking his baby was still in its cot.

I looked at Mick and whispered, "That's good news, but the poor chap is going to wake up with one hell of a bloody headache!" Mick just smiled back knowingly!

So, my first real fire attended, weeks of struggle brought to fruition, my thoughts went back to that very first day of arrival months before.

As I pulled up outside the imposing entrance of the Fire Service Headquarters to start the first day of three months-plus of residential training, little did I know what was ahead of me! This was going to be life changing in many ways. It was going to push me to my physical and mental limits as well as testing my emotions. Life was about to change and never be the same again. Not just my life but also that of my wife and at that time our young daughter.

Yes, I was about to become a firefighter, well I was about to start the process at least, but this story didn't begin here, it began months before when a young twenty-three-year-old Insurance Salesman looked at his life and thought is this it? Can I really do this for the next thirty or forty years? That thought filled me with dread. It was a working from home day in the life of an Insurance Salesman, a day to sort things out for the week. All interesting stuff as you can imagine!

The phone rang and a long conversation with my manager continued for quite some time. I put the phone down and sighed, I looked at my wife who was standing nearby holding our young daughter in her arms. "Janine, guess what? Jeff says well done for my sales last week, but they've upped the bloody targets for the next three months!"

Janine just looked at me holding our little bundle of joy who had arrived just three months before and with that knowing look. "Nothing changes, does it?" she replied.

She was right; nearly three years I'd been doing this job and although I loved meeting the people and sometimes, yes, the buzz of a sale, it was, as with all sales jobs, you're only as good as your last sale, nothing else really mattered. I sat there pondering my situation for a minute. Then the call of the stinkiest nappy in the world hit me.

"Your turn," Janine said with great delight, handing over our little bundle of joy to me. A seed had been planted in my mind several months earlier that was about to sprout its young shoots.

I had been invited to come along with a youth group that I helped with for a visit to our local fire station to have a look around. We arrived at the station with our young group in tow.

"Can we squirt the water?" shouted one young lad who stood with us in great excitement.

The smartly dressed officer who met us at the door looked at the young chap, seeing his eagerness. "We'll see what we can do," and gave him a knowing smirk.

"Yes!" said the young lad, looking excitedly at those around him.

"First I need to go through a few safety points before we look around," continued the Station Officer. He beckoned us to follow him into the heart of the station where we could all see the fireman's pole. At this point there was a gaggle of chatter and excitement from all the children and yes, the adults who were there seemed equally as excited by seeing this. Who knew the effects a tube of steel could have?

He gathered us in a group next to a printer and a row of telephones all on a table with lots of maps of the local area on the wall above. "Ok, everyone welcome, as you know this is a working fire station and we could get a shout at any time."

"What's a shout?" asked one of the group.

"Yes, sorry, that's what we call a call out to an incident and if that happens you will all hear this sound." He leant over to a microphone next to the telephones and pressed the button underneath it and speaking into it, said, "Test call, take no action". This came over the loudspeakers so everyone in the station heard it. He then picked up a big bright red telephone and spoke into that. "Hello, control, can you send a test call out through, we've got some young visitors."

As soon as he had finished his sentence, the printer started whirring and what seemed the loudest beeping sound ever came over all the speakers in the station and got louder and louder. A buzz of smiles and giggles came over the group and I must say what seemed like a little burst of adrenalin came over me. I thought what it must be like to hear that sound, not knowing what kind of emergency you could be going to and the fact that it could go off at any time, you just didn't know. The Station Officer continued by pressing the button with the microphone again; "test complete," he said then looked at us all. "That's so everyone knows if it goes off again, it's a real call."

He continued chatting about the station, how many worked there and was partly through his conversation when one of the young girls in the group pointed out the elephant in the room, this being the same question on many of their young minds. "Can we go down the fireman's pole?" while the expression on her face could hide her inner thoughts being, he's going to say no.

"Yes! Yes!" the group joined in.

"We're not supposed to…" he hesitated. "So if anyone asks you, it has never happened," said the Officer with a wry smile on his face. "No messing around and do as you're instructed, ok?" he said, looking around at everyone, his eyebrows raised, a time pre health and safety and risk assessments. He pressed the button on the microphone again. "John, can you come and give me a hand?" came the announcement over the tannoy, and John soon appeared. He was a big guy with a smile just as big. John went to the floor above where there was a pair of doors which swung open with a noisy clunk. We all gathered near the bottom so we all could see. At the bottom of the pole was a padded mat.

"John is going to show you how to come down the pole properly, and if anyone hurts themselves the story is, you slipped down the stairs; only joking, but no injuries please, I can't be doing with all the extra paperwork. Ok?" He said this with a hint of irony knowing everything would be fine as long as we didn't mess around.

John then showed us that the technique was not to grab hold with just our hands but to grip hard with our legs around the pole. He came down the pole with no hands holding it at all, just his legs wrapped around. Again, a big cheer came from the group.

"Right, you lot, hands and legs when you do it, I was just showing that it should be your legs that slow you down, not just your hands."

One by one, with John at the floor above and the officer at the bottom of the pole, we all came down. Some with very screechy sounds as they held on too tightly. Particularly the girls who were wearing skirts and had bare legs. Great fun was had by all though. Our tour continued on.

"Ok, follow me into the engine house," said the officer.

We followed eagerly on into a long room with bright red vehicles parked neatly in a row. It smelt strongly of both diesel and oil. "Ok, we are going to look around the appliances now."

"I thought they are fire engines?" someone piped up quizzically.

"They are," said the officer. "But as you can see, we have two that look similar and the one on the end which is completely different–" he pointed at this big, long vehicle which looked to have a massive silver ladder on the top which ran the full length of the vehicle, even protruding over the cab at the front. "That's called a turntable ladder, and its ladder goes up to just over one hundred feet."

"Wow," I said. The thought in my head of having to climb up it. I had seen these, of course, but at that time only as a toy vehicle that I had played with as a child and occasionally when they were driving around the town. As well as footage of fires with some poor chap at the top, pointing a jet of water.

"So as these vehicles are all different, we call them appliances, but they all have their own specific names and their own number," the officer continued.

We were shown around the appliances. The first is called a Water Ladder because it too had a big ladder on it. Not quite as tall, he said, but enough to get up to the fourth floor of a building. Then the Water Tender; this looked very similar but with a smaller wooden ladder. The officer showed us around the fire engines with all the hose and equipment they used. Explaining that as firemen it wasn't just fires that they attended (again at the time this took place, the term "firefighter" to include both genders wasn't in common use! Things were going to change thankfully very quickly).

"Time is passing on and one of the lads is cooking us a very nice curry for our supper tonight," continued the officer. There was indeed a lovely smell coming from some other part of the station. He explained that later in the evening, as they were on duty until the next morning, the whole watch would be having a curry together for their supper. Food, I was to find out later, was a crucial part of the firefighter's day.

Before that he said it was time for the watch to do what they called 'Drill'. "Right, everyone, I'm going to get all the watch out in a minute to do a short drill you can all watch, just stay over there out of the way–" pointing to a part of the station yard out of the way but where we could see all that was going on. We all gathered in this spot, again eager to see what was going to happen next. The officer walked back to the room we had been in at the start of our tour and over the loudspeaker came his booming voice. "Blue Watch dress for drill." At that point firefighters seemed to appear from various points around the station and made their way into the engine room where all the vehicles were all parked neatly side by side. Putting on their boots and pulling up yellow trousers with straps over their shoulders, then grabbing their tunics and helmets in what looked like a choreographed break dance. A couple of firefighters went to the back of the engine room and pulled on big ropes that hung down with big knots on the end. When they did this, it caused the big red doors to spring wide-open to allow the vehicles which had started their engines to reverse out into the back yard. Over in the corner of the yard was a very tall tower made of brick and concrete. Six floors each with openings front and sides. Once all three appliances had reversed in a line, the drivers switched off their engines and joined the rest of the firefighters who had stood in an orderly line at the rear of each vehicle. The officer who had been showing us around that evening was clearly in charge. He had got dressed into his working clothes, but unlike the others he put on a white helmet. Everyone else wore yellow but two or three of the firefighters had yellow ones but with black stripes that went around the bottom of them.

"Blue Watch the drill will be..." instructed the now white helmeted officer. All the firefighters looked on and stood there at ease with both hands behind their backs and legs slightly apart. It struck me at this point as to how military and regimented everything was. The officer continued to address the men lined up "… to get a jet working from the turntable ladder into the fifth-floor window, this is to be fed from the open water tank from the water tender." He hesitated for a moment, looked at the ten men stood in a line in front of him. They seemed to nod in unison. "Drill as detailed, get to work," he shouted in a strong authoritative voice. At that point it seemed like someone had fired a starting pistol. The firefighters ran in all directions, some jumping onto the fire engine, engines starting, two ran to the back of the engines, one to each vehicle, waving their arms around using a sign language with their arms that clearly the driver seemed to understand. Walking backwards until the vehicles were in their correct positions. Lockers were thrust open. Firefighters grabbing equipment. Hose and large tubes which were connected to the back of the appliance. The children strained to see what was going on in excitement, this was clearly fun to watch, and all were having a great time.

The turntable ladder was placed near to the large tower and large legs were pulled out at each corner of the vehicle. This was to support the vehicle. Then one of the firefighters climbed on to the platform at the back where there was a seat with a control panel with levers on it. Moving the levers, the big silver ladder moved upwards, pointing at an angle towards the window higher up in the tower, spinning around in the direction of the tower. It then extended upwards with a clunk, clunk, clunk sound as the ladder gradually got longer and longer. Higher and higher until it was at the height of the fifth-floor window. As this was happening the other firefighters had been running around, big tubes at the back of the fire engine going into a hole in the ground. Others had run around with large rolls of circular hose that they held at chest height, holding them with both hands, running forward and leaving a line of flat hose on the floor behind them.

The officer came over to us stood in a line we had formed so we could spectate the scene. "All ok?" he gestured to us. "Enjoying yourselves?"

An answer of "Yes!" returned in unison.

Various things were being communicated between the busy firefighters then the one sat on the seat controlling the ladder suddenly raised his right arm and shouted, "Water on!" in a loud voice that was nearly drowned out by the sound of engines revving.

Two other firefighters repeated the same command, shouting loudly. At this point a helmeted face popped out from the back of the engine with the big tubes that went into the hole. Giving everyone a cheeky smile, he then stood to attention so all could see him and repeated the up-stretched arm with a clenched fist and shouted back "Water on".

Disappearing back behind the vehicle; then the noise of the engine increased and the flat hose that lay on the ground erupted into life, filling visibly with water under pressure. All eyes in the group following it as it raced and snaked across the ground, becoming solid as the water filled it, reaching the big turntable ladder in no time. A few seconds later a loud crackling noise could be heard at the top of the ladder and then the water gushed out of a small tube that was pointing into the window. So much water poured it soon ran down inside the tower forming a waterfall from floor to floor as it cascaded its way down the tower to the yard and then disappearing into a drain in the corner of the yard.

The officer in charge then walked over to a firefighter who seemed to be one of the youngest looking, he spoke into the side of the young man's face for a few moments. Then the young firefighter turned on his heels and ran off in the other direction to one of the lockers on the side of the turntable ladder. He pulled out a big strap looking thing and put it around his waist. Climbing onto the back of the turntable ladder, he then proceeded to climb up it, slowly but confidently, until he reached the top which swayed with his weight. My thought at that point was that I wasn't sure I could do that. It seemed so precarious and high! To be perfectly honest, I wasn't great with heights. Or to be completely honest, I had a strong fear of them.

"Knock off and make up!" came the booming voice of the officer. Again, in the same quick precision, the firefighter proceeded to make everything that they had used disappear back into its orderly place.

The officer came back over to us and the hand of the little lad who had asked the question earlier sprang up into the air. "Excuse me, I thought you said we could squirt some water?"

The officer looked back at him, smiling again. "Oh I haven't forgotten; when the guys have finished, you're going to be using something a bit special."

Eager little faces looking at each other in excitement, as well as the children's.

Everything put away, the firefighters again formed an orderly line and stood at attention, feet together, arms by their sides. The officer stood facing them. "Good drill, lads" he said. "Go get that curry sorted, dismiss." In unison the men all turned to their right, stamped their feet together and dispersed.

"Ok," said the officer, looking back at us. "Who's for squirting some water?" To a big cheer he then started the engine again, opened a locker at the back of the fire engine; inside was a big drum with a long thin hose wound in it and what looked like a gun on the end. Taking it in his hand, he started to describe to us all what it was.

"This is a high-pressure hose reel, and it squirts water a long way and at a very high pressure," he said – and it did. Everyone got to have a go with a few ending up slightly damp but very happy.

So, this was the seed that had been planted in my mind that had clearly been gestating over the last few months and that had come to a head with my current work frustrations. I had a young family, undertaken a mortgage, and had responsibilities. But the thought of the next thirty or forty years doing what I was doing now continued to fill me with utter dread! Yes, it was time for a complete change.

So, 1986 was the year that I decided that this change of direction would commence, hopefully. But it would be a further eighteen months until I would find myself outside the Fire Training Centre ready to go in and start.

It was eighteen long months of application forms, attending fire stations for written tests, manual dexterity tests, maths and English tests. One of these took place at a fire station in a large Yorkshire City. We were all there, smartly dressed, all wearing our best suits for the tests. As we were being shown through to the room we were going to take the tests in, a group of firefighters were sat in comfy chairs. Obviously spotting us one of them piped up: "Here we go, another lot who's been watching bloody London's Burning." His colleagues all laughed. He wasn't wrong though; I had watched it. It was the sarcasm in his tone I didn't pick up on straight away. It would be a long time later I was to realise his point. Being a fireman (from this point onwards I will use the proper and more up to date and enlightened term of "Firefighter" as what had been seen as a male-only career was about to start to change, even if only slowly at this point in time. The first female firefighter in our Brigade was about to be recruited at the same time as me) – yes, being a firefighter and real firefighting had very little to do with what was portrayed and represented on TV programmes like London's Burning and, I will say, the majority of firefighting portrayed on TV and Film is nothing like the reality!

So, tests passed, I was one of the lucky ones to be invited to Headquarters for interview. Again, suited and booted I sat outside one of the interview rooms in a corridor nervously waiting to be called in. The door swung open and in front of me, a big man dressed in black with silver buttons and pips all over his shoulders spoke. "Mr Cooke?"

I nervously replied, "Yes, sir."

"Come in."

I followed him in, closing the door behind me. What confronted me was a large wide desk with two further fully dressed officers seated before me. The officer who had called me in went to join his colleagues behind the large wooden desk. I walked up to the desk, stood to attention and reached out my hand for them to shake. I didn't know if this was appropriate or not. One grabbed hold of my hand and I don't know if he was making a point or not, but he squeezed it that hard I nearly said "Ouch!"; he turned out to be Mr Nasty Officer. I'm not sure if this was a planned tried and tested way to conduct an interview or from the Fire Service book of intimidation – oh how times have changed in such a relatively short period.

"So, Mr Cooke, you want to join the fire service – can you tell me why?" began Mr Nice Officer.

The questions kept coming alternating from Mr Nice to Mr Nasty, interjecting with the odd nod and smile from who I will call Mr Indifferent. This went on for what seemed like ages. Then suddenly Mr Nice Officer said, "Ok, Mr Cooke, would you mind waiting outside whilst we discuss your interview."

"Of course," I said. "Thank you for your time in seeing me."

As I sat down outside to wait, another smartly dressed young man was already sat there on the seat next to me.

"You waiting to go in for interview?" I asked.

"Yes," he replied. "How did it go?" he asked.

"Alright I think?" I leaned in closer and whispered to him. "The one on the right is a bit of a nasty bugger!"

"Ok," he said with a slightly puzzled look.

"I think he was trying to intimidate me," I whispered with false bravado.

"I think he just wants to put you on the spot."

He'd done a bloody good job, I thought to myself.

We both sat there for a while nervously waiting. Then the door swung open again. "Mr Cooke would you come back in please?"

I followed him in.

"Sit down."

I sat down.

Then Mr Nasty Officer reached his hand over the desk at me. "Welcome to the Fire Service, Mr Cooke," he said with a pleasant smile on his face that I clearly hadn't seen up until that point. "Thank you," I said excitedly.

"Just two more things you have to do."

I looked at him quizzically.

"You need to go up to see the Brigade Doctor now and he will carry out a final medical and sign you as fit to continue, then you'll go and do a fireman's carry with a live casualty outside on the Parade Ground."

I nodded, and he continued. "Once you've completed these you will be allocated a Training Course when one becomes available."

Not quite there yet then, I thought to myself. I shook all their hands and thanked them again, then walked out and wished the young guy outside all the best.

"I think I'm in," I said to him.

"What do you mean?" he replied.

I told him what was going to happen to me next. The funny thing is he also passed his interview shortly after, and once we had both seen the doctor with his ok, we were taken to the parade ground and shown how to do a firefighter's lift. So, both dressed in suits we took it in turns to carry each other the 100 yards to a cone and back again. This all took place whilst next to us on the parade ground, a training course was in progress where firefighters were running around putting up ladders with an awful lot of shouting going on. We both looked on and I'm sure my new colleague was thinking exactly the same as me. That that would be us soon. Yes, I thought to myself, after all the hardship in the application process that was it, I was in.

5

Here I was pulling into the entrance to The Fire Training Centre to start my training after having to wait for four months from that interview for a training course to become available and for the money to become available in the Brigade to train a new set of recruits. It was a strange time to start, it was between Christmas and New Year's Eve. The Brigade for the first time had decided to do a four-day induction course before the residential course started in the New Year.

My brother and his family had been staying with us over the Christmas period. We were discussing the change coming up with each other and having to attend this induction course over the Christmas holiday time.

"Oh, it will just be to show you around, get your bearings," he said.

"Do you reckon?"

"Yes, let you know what's going to happen in the New Year," said my brother reassuringly.

"I'm not sure, it all seems a bit strange you know, the timing!" I replied. "Why not just start in the New Year?"

The letter that had come telling me which course I would be on mentioned, of course, that this four-day Induction was being introduced. No explanation was given as to why. I was about to find out the real reason for it.

We were all directed into a large lecture theatre, and there we all sat in rows gradually increasing in numbers, until we reached what looked like about forty of us. Then a very smartly dressed uniformed officer came in and walked down to the lectern at the front. He stood there with red braiding around his shoulder that looped under his arm and went down to his waist, shirt neatly ironed with creases down the front and arms. He stood, gripped either side of the lectern with both hands and started to address us all. "Ladies and Gents, welcome."

I looked around; I hadn't realised that any women were on the course at that point. Then I spotted one young lady who had her hair pulled tightly back into a bun at the back of her head. We had been told in the letter we had received that men's hair was to be short back and sides. Ladies, obviously, as she had hers neatly fastened in a bun. I thought that she must be feeling slightly outnumbered being the only female on the course.

"Ok, I will be calling out your names in groups of six," he continued. "You will be given a squad number, and you will remain in that squad for the duration of the course," he said, continuing to hold the lectern firmly with both hands at either side. "Once you are in your squad you will be led out with your squad officer to get kitted out." He looked around the room at everyone. "Understand?" he questioned.

Some of us nodded, some said "Yes".

Raising his voice in a very loud tone: "When you are asked a question from an officer you will answer in the affirmative or negative immediately followed by Sir in my case," he boomed, pointing at the two pips on his shoulder. "Do you understand?"

"Yes, sir!" came the immediate response in unison.

"If it's a Leading Firefighter," he continued, "with one bar on his shoulder, you will refer to him as LF, two bars then he is referred to as Sub, short for Sub-Officer."

The guy sat next to me whispered very quietly, "Have we joined the bloody army?"

I just looked at him and smiled, but the same thought had entered my mind. Off we all marched to stores to be kitted out. Big yellow helmet, black fire tunic, plastic yellow wet legs, t-shirts and a blue bib and brace to be worn under our fire kit. This was called our working rig, but we all looked like extras from a wild west film or that we had all joined Dexy's Midnight Runners. A pale blue shirt with epaulettes to go with it, but with no writing on them. A black clip-on tie, black shoes which would have to be buffed up shiny black on the toes. Shorts and black old-fashioned pumps to be worn for PT. We were told our full kit, which would include our full undress uniform, would be given to us later. The tone and attitude of all the officers was short and brusque.

We were all shown how to parade, all in straight lines, each member of the squad one arm's length apart. Each squad equal distance apart. Either at ease with legs apart, arms crossed behind our backs or to attention with legs together, arms stiff to our sides, hands clenched, thumbs facing to the front. Chin up. Marching would come later.

All this was taught to us by someone who looked and sounded like a regimental Sergeant Major. He even had a yard stick under his arm, "Stand still the front line," he bellowed, pointing his stick along the front line. "Dress right the front line!" he bellowed again, watching and pointing whilst we all shuffled, right arms outstretched, touching the person to our right until we achieved a line he was happy with. Once he was happy with our straight lines, "Stand still the front line!" he bellowed again. This went on with all the rows until he was happy with how we looked.

We were ordered that if at any time we were on the outside of the training centre buildings we were to either run at double pace or to be marched around by an officer. No walking under any circumstances.

So, the first day over, home I went and walked into the house. "A bloody nice introduction," I said to my brother who was sat down comfortably reclined in his chair. "A gentle introduction into what would be going to happen?" I said exasperated.

"Tough day then?" he replied.

"I'll say," I said, sitting down. "I'm not sure I'm on the right course, I think I may have joined the Bloody Army by mistake!" I said sarcastically.

We both laughed. But the truth was I was in a little bit of shell shock about it all. I wasn't the only one. Two people had left the course by early afternoon on that first day, stating that it wasn't for them.

So, I'd had a taste on the first day as to the reasons why they were running this induction course. With two gone, it was obviously to eliminate, by various means necessary, those who they thought couldn't last the course as soon as they possibly could. A pattern was going to appear over the next three days. This was to push us to see if we had any problems with discipline and authority. Any problems with heights, claustrophobia, physical fitness, and see if we were the type of people who could work well as part of a team. Would we follow orders without question?

Today's test on day two would be claustrophobia. And that was to be by the use of what was called 'the crawl'. The crawl was a series of cages, obstacles interlinked with small openings, tunnels, tubes, drains and passages. Firstly, we were taken into a classroom with individual desks and in front of each desk hung a breathing apparatus set minus the air cylinder.

"Ok, gents, find a desk and stand behind it," spoke one of the officers. "From this point on," he continued, "when you enter into any classroom you will find a seat under each of the desks, you will not sit down but stand behind it and wait until one of the instructors tells you to be seated." Looking around: "Understand?" he questioned. "If you are told to go into a classroom and be seated you will stand as soon as an officer comes into a room."

"Yes, sir" came the automatic response.

"Today, you are going to be shown how to set up your Breathing Apparatus Sets or BA, so that we can carry out today's drill." Holding a set in his hands, he continued. "This will be just a basic instruction now so you can wear it for today's exercise, you will get to know this piece of equipment like the backs of your hands as your life will literally depend upon it." He continued describing step by step setting it up as we attentively followed each step.

Once we had set them up ready to use, we put them onto our backs ready to put the face masks onto our faces. I couldn't believe how heavy they were. Then putting our face masks on, pulling the straps tight, quick sharp intake of breath to get the air to flow and then turning the knob on the mask so it showed a cross which meant positive pressure. This meant air came easily on demand. The room sounded like it had been filled with 20 Darth Vaders all breathing heavily. We were then shown how to shut the sets down, so we were ready to continue.

"On another day you will be shown fully how we test everything before we use it and again after we have used it." He smiled at us all. "You'll soon realise that everything in the fire service is tested and signed for again and again."

Lifting a book up so we could all see. "Each set has a number and a book which corresponds to that number; you will be shown how it is tested, signed for and signed and tested again after it's been used."

A lasting memory of this time is one of smell. The BA block as it was known was a building on its own with classrooms next to a large gymnasium. The classrooms and gym were above 'the crawl', which was a complex underground system, one I was about to be so rudely introduced to. This connected with a complex of sewer pipes, access hatches and eventually to a large building next to it called the 'Smoke House'.

The smoke house was a solid building of brick and concrete with concrete floors, filled with lots of rooms, passages, stairs and raking ladders. Fires could be lit in these rooms and an unlimited number of fire scenarios could be set up. More of this later, but back to that memory which has never gone and one that would return every time in the future I was to revisit this place, 'the smell'! It was the acrid smell of smoke and the aftereffects of fire. It must be the fact that so many difficult exercises would be carried out here over the coming weeks, that smell would bring memories back of the good times and the bad times experienced here.

Back in the classroom we had been split into three groups, with two squads in each group. Whilst we were going to be experiencing the delights of breathing apparatus, the other groups would be out on the drill square doing ladders or basic hose running and pump drills.

"Gents, get dressed into your fire kit and then straight back in here, put your breathing sets on and your facemasks around your neck."

At this point Karen wasn't part of the group doing BA with us, but the instructors would always make a point of addressing us as Ladies and Gents when she was present. Raising his arms in the air. "Chop, chop." We all quickly came back dressed in our fire kit, put our BA sets on and stood behind our desks. The Subo came back in himself fully dressed followed by two other leading firefighters also fully dressed in their fire kit. What followed would be something that would happen in the future many, many times.

"Before we start the exercise we will be going through a briefing and a safety briefing." He switched on an acetate projector. This was long before the days of computers and digital projectors. On the white board an image of a plan of the crawl, pipes and tunnels and a building plan full of rooms. Pointing at the plan, he then explained what the exercise would be. Once we had started up wearing our breathing apparatus, we were to follow a guideline that had already been laid and to keep following it until our air ran out. He explained that a warning whistle on our air sets would sound before we ran out of air. This one time he said we were to ignore it and were to just carry on.

"Is everyone fit and well?" he asked us. "Are there any reasons why anyone cannot continue? If so, please raise your hand now," looking around the room at each one of us to see any response. "Is everyone fit to continue?"

"Yes, Sub" came the group response.

So off we went following him outside the building and down the flight of stairs to the start of the crawl.

We all lined up at the entrance of the crawl which was a two-foot-high square door on the floor.

"Right, gents, start up your BA sets in pairs and follow the guideline laid. It will be pitch black most of the time and there will be obstacles along the way."

We all stood there hesitantly in line, the first two starting their sets up with the usual 'Darth Vader' sound of breathing.

"As soon as they get in, start up the next two," he said, pointing at the next two in line. The first two got down on their hands and knees and began their journey into the darkness. At that point the next two started. Then came my turn with the guy next to me.

"What's your name?" I said to him, thinking life would be easier when communicating with each other.

"Phil," he replied.

"Mark," I said to him.

Phil was a large guy and would later become a great friend and help whilst at training school.

"I'll take the lead," Phil said to me.

"No problem," I replied.

To be honest I was quite pleased. At that point I didn't know that Phil was very used to this. He was already a retained firefighter with the Brigade. (That's a part-time firefighter who is on call from work or home. These are mainly based in small towns or villages that don't need the same level of fire cover as a town or city.) This was a piece of information that he later confided with me. But one he didn't want many to know as he thought that the instructors would use it against him and add extra pressure on him. They obviously already knew, but the fact that he acted and behaved as one of us and not as a 'know it all' made the instructors treat him the same as everyone else. So, in we went on hands and knees crawling into the dark.

"You Ok, Mark?" Phil asked.

"Yes, right behind you," I replied.

The guideline that we were to follow was a type of thin rope which had been laid tied off above our heads every few feet. On our BA sets was a small line attached to a pouch that could be pulled out to 1.25 metres or five metres. This had a snap hook on the end which we clipped onto the guideline as we went along. We had entered what appeared to be a section of metal cages with gaps just big enough to squeeze through, that alternated with left turns then right turns that seemed to go on and on. The further we proceeded the darker it became as the light from the small entrance retreated, further and further away. It also became noisier as more of us entered into the crawl with the sounds of breathing and people shouting instructions to each other.

"We've got a right-hand turn with a small gap to get through!" Phil shouted at me.

It was now completely pitch black and progress was made by feel alone.

"Ok," I replied.

"When I'm through I'll shout and bang on the cage side," he came back.

"Ok?" I grunted.

At that point I had maintained a constant relationship with Phil's fire boots. It entered my mind that if you suffered from claustrophobia, the action of wearing the Breathing Apparatus in the darkness and confined space would activate anyone's phobia

– again this was obviously part of the plan which was to soon gain another victim.

I proceeded to follow Phil; occasionally there would be a sudden light shined at us, illuminating the whole area then just as quickly disappear, producing what seemed an even blacker darkness.

Monitoring proceedings were the instructors. Our progress was watched through little viewing ports with their torches. Phil and I had been in the crawl maybe about ten minutes when a commotion erupted behind us with lots of loud shouting, banging and rattling of the metal cages. We could see torch lights suddenly come on as this was happening, but it was too far behind us to make anything out.

"Everyone, carry on through the crawl" came the shout of one of the instructors through a viewing point.

At this point Phil turned towards me and with a frustrated voice shouted, "There's a great pile of bloody tyres in front of me!"

"Right," I replied.

"I'll have to pull a couple back so we can make a gap big enough to crawl over the others."

"Ok, I'll move back a bit." I reversed from Phil's boots which incidentally my head had continued to make contact with several times, now to find the space being filled by a tyre being shoved into it.

"You Ok, Mark?"

"Yes, no probs," I replied sarcastically.

We both clambered over the other tyres and continued.

We had reached the end of the crawl where there was another small doorway as an exit. As we came out into a long corridor our instructor shone his torch at us. "Gents, go along this corridor and on the left is a sewer pipe, climb in and follow it until you receive more instructions." He pointed his torch down the corridor to the pipe entrance. "How much air do you both have?" he asked us. We both lifted our gauges and pointed them at him so he could see. "Plenty, right carry on," he said.

Down the corridor in the opposite direction, we could see several instructors with their torches on with two firefighters, one of whom had his face mask off and was bent over with his hands on his knees. I could just make out what one of the instructors was saying to him. "We know this kind of thing can happen, but you need to get straight back in and carry on."

"Hurry up, you two," the instructor next to us shouted.

Phil and I carried on, back on our hands and knees and into the round sewer pipe. Again, as soon as the torch light went out it became pitch black.

"This is hard on the old bloody knees," said Phil.

He was not wrong, crawling down a round concrete sewer pipe wasn't the most comfortable of experiences. Along we went for what seemed to be ages before it became lighter. We caught up with the other teams that were in front of us. All you could hear was heavy breathing, muffled voices and a voice shouting "Climb up, one at once!" There was a backlog of firefighters all on their hands and knees waiting to stand up and climb up and out via a vertical shaft which had metal foot holds one step at a time up to the round exit at the top where the instructor's head peered over shouting "Next". The problem was the footholds were also the handholds and the vertical pipe was only just wide enough to squeeze up through with breathing apparatus on your back.

At this point the sounds of whistles going off one after the other became deafening. All breathing apparatus are fitted with this feature. Our later training would be crucial in teaching us how to monitor our air consumption and that it was vital to be out in the open air before our whistles went off. But for the purpose of this exercise though, we carried on until we ran out of air.

The instructor was becoming slightly exasperated by the speed of our exit though and the fact that so many whistles were starting to go off. "Come on, get your arses into gear" came his bellowing voice down the shaft. Eventually we made our way into the outside world again, popping up one at a time, the equivalent of firefighter meerkats.

Phil and I gathered with the other emergent firefighters, took off our masks and gathered into what was to become a familiar position, 'the firefighter circle'. Post any exercise or incident you will see this the world over. Firefighters all in a circle facing each other, discussing what has just happened. The discussion soon went to the incident we had partially witnessed in the corridor part of the crawl.

"Did you see what had happened in the crawl to Dave?" one of the firefighters in the group asked us. He continued, "Dave completely freaked out part way through the crawl, they had to drag him out."

We were later informed by one of the instructors back in the classroom for the debrief that as we had heard, Dave had struggled with the claustrophobia. He had been told that this can happen, especially if this is the first time you're put in that position. He was given every opportunity to go back straight away and complete the crawl and was asked three times. He had refused so there was no alternative – that was the end of his firefighting career.

7

The following day it was crew change round again. Those who had been doing ladders were to be having the delights of Breathing Apparatus. Today's delight for me would be the one that worried me the most, 'heights'! Yes, it was time for ladders.

The first ladder would be the 'Lacon' ladder. This was an alloy ladder that was in three extendable sections that went to approximately forty-five feet. It had two large poles attached on either side that were used to extend it and bring it back down. It needed four people to operate it. This is the ladder you will still see on most fire appliances in the UK today. But today wasn't about learning to operate the ladder, it was about climbing it and being confident at height.

A little secret? I may have mentioned this, heights had been a real problem for me and a real worry. I had never been confident with heights and an incident at home a few weeks earlier had done nothing to help this. "I'm going to paint the weatherboard on the side of the house," I said to Janine. "It's in dire need!" Ladders borrowed from a neighbour and pitched up to the peak of the side of the house, off I climbed. Fine at first, then the nearer the ladder got to the house and the higher I got the more I slowed down. The ground seemed twice as far away and my confidence evaporated. The thought entered my head "What are you doing joining the Fire Brigade? It's nothing but ladders and bloody heights!!" This was a fear I had to conquer, one I needed to be honest with myself about. If I was to become a firefighter, I had to overcome it. But as I was to find out, it wasn't going to be instant.

Whenever a ladder is used in the fire service there always has to be someone 'footing it' – that is, to have someone at the bottom with one foot on the ground and one foot on the ladder. This is to make sure that the ladder is safe and that someone is watching what is going on. In the Fire Service you never get onto a ladder either from the top or the bottom unless it has someone footing it.

"Cooke?"

"Yes, Sub," I replied.

The Subo pointing at me: "Foot the ladder for me so I can show you all what I want you to do."

At that point we were all lined up in a row, stood at ease. I jogged over to the foot of the ladder which was at full extension against the tower in the middle of the drill square. He pointed at the beam that ran horizontally at the base of the ladder. "Stick one foot on that," he said, pointing at the bottom of the ladder.

"The rung," I said.

"What the bloody hell is a rung!" he shouted at me. "You're not a bloody window cleaner?"

"Sorry, Sub!" I replied sheepishly. But thinking what the hell is it then, I always knew you climbed up the rungs of a ladder. I was to find out so much in the fire service was different.

"It's called a round not a rung," he continued, "and these things going up on either side to the top are called strings."

"Yes, Sub!" I replied quickly, not wanting to attract any more embarrassing attention. As I have said, so many things in the fire service, terms, commands etc. I would learn were different. In this case based on the Navy term of the 'Strings' and 'Rounds' to be found on ships' rigging. So, with me footing the ladder, the instructor then started to climb up, explaining as he went the correct way to do so. Right foot, right arm up one round at the same time. Then left foot and left arm, again up one round. He continued this climbing up to nearly forty foot in height to the third extension. He was now shouting down his instructions so we could all hear him. I just looked up the ladder thinking it was a bloody long way up. But his next instruction was to make that feeling even worse. "OK at this point." He had stopped with both feet on the same round and both arms outstretched again on the same round. "Hold tightly onto the ladder with both hands." At that point he lifted one leg off the ladder and two rounds above the other leg put his whole leg through so that it was on the other side of the ladder. His knee was bent over the round. "When you're in this position," he shouted. "Take the whole weight of your body on this right leg, let go with both hands and lean completely backwards." There he was backwards, viewing the world from an upside-down position, his body arched in a reverse crucifix position held on by his legs. Yes, you can imagine as to what my thoughts were at this point. That horrible sinking feeling hit me right in the stomach, my heart rate rose, and I felt slightly nauseous. I thought to myself I'm going to have to do this myself soon. Un-arching his body holding back onto the ladder with his hands he climbed back down the ladder stood next to me. "Easy as that," he said. "Right, Cooke, you're here already off you go." My heart sank, but as I had previously said and thought, if I didn't conquer this fear then it would be my career as a firefighter coming to an end. It was now or never, but I knew I could not show any of the fear I was feeling inside.

I stood on the bottom round both feet and arms outstretched. "Off you climb," said the Sub and off I went, trying to imitate the same technique to climb as the Subo had shown us. Surprisingly I was to find this technique easy to master, others were to find it a mystery, legs and arms completely out of sync, a bit like the mastery of marching. Some always struggling with a version of the 'Spotty Dog' that is legs and arms not alternating but the left arm moving in the same direction as the left leg. The right side doing the same. This imitating the Spotty Dog puppet from black and white Children's TV – showing my age now! I concentrated so intently on my technique of climbing the ladder that it seemed to focus my mind. As I climbed one round at a time, I kept my head looking straight ahead, but in my peripheral vision I could see the ground getting further away. All this did was increase my feelings of vulnerability. "Keep breathing normally – you can do this," I voiced in my head. The fact that I had a crowd of fellow prospective firefighters watching me had the required effect. Off I went higher and higher until I heard the shout of "Rest!" (Again, the fire service can't just say stop it has to have its own command).

"Right, Cooke, take a leg lock there," he shouted up at me. I grabbed the round with both hands, hanging on for dear life as I lifted my right leg up to put it through, once in position. "Right lean right back with your arms outstretched." I leant back to what I thought was a horrendously insecure position. "Cooke, further back. I want to see the whites of your eyes." The feeling was if I leaned any further back, I might as well just do a bloody backflip! And as regards the 'whites of my eyes!' you'll see brown trousers in a minute I thought to myself. There I was, arched backwards, hanging off a ladder looking at the Drill Square and everything in it upside down. Funny way to earn a living came to mind? Legs shaking. "Right, Cooke, get back down!" chirped the Subo. I was glad that was over with, but it had actually boosted my confidence such that even at this point in time heights wasn't my favourite pastime, but I knew I could do it.

Then in the afternoon parked, next to the seven-storey tower, was the large turntable ladder, yes just like the one on my visit to the fire station. This had been brought from the nearest station purely for our pleasure. I think at that time the Brigade had half a dozen dotted at stations around the county. We all lined up stood at ease whilst the operator pitched the ladder up to the top of the tower. My mind flipped back all those months ago on the visit to our local station and the thoughts I had had as to whether I could climb up to the top as I had watched that young lad months before. Yes, I had conquered the ladder earlier, but this was in a different league. That question was about to be answered.

When we were all lined up the leading firefighter addressed us. "OK, as you can see this afternoon you are all going to climb the turntable ladder and when you're at the top you will be instructed by the Subo the correct way to get off the ladder and onto the top of the tower."

We all responded, "Yes LF!"

"He will have a quick chat with you, then tell you to come back down via the internal raking ladders on each floor. (Raking ladders are vertical metal ladders attached permanently to the wall, usually accessed through a hole in the floor. A staple of every fire station, smoke house etc.) I stood there watching as several of my colleagues ascended one at a time; once they got to the top, we could see the instructor gesticulating to each firefighter what he wanted them to do. From where we stood this appeared a very strange procedure. There also seemed to be quite a time gap after getting off to the radio message being sent to the instructor on the ground of, "Ok send the next one up". Finally, my turn came, so off I climbed. The further up I got the more the ladder flexed. It hadn't been rested onto the top of the tower, but a gap of about a foot had been left on purpose. It was quite disconcerting, the ladder moving with your body movement the further I climbed. It also got a lot thinner nearer the top as well. The ground just got further and further away. My heart was pounding but again I was determined this fear had to be conquered. When I got to the top the ladder it had been extended several rounds above the top of the tower.

"Right, climb so that your feet are level with the top of the tower," the instructor commanded me. The top had a metal railing running around it with a drop of around three feet on the inside to the floor. "Bring your left hand over to the right-hand side of this round in front of you and put your right hand around the back of the ladder and grab the same round," he instructed. Once I had done that: "Keep your left leg on the ladder and with your right leg stamp on the top of the ledge three times". What on earth for, I thought to myself. I was later to find out this is done because in a fire and rescue situation you don't know how safe the structure is and by stamping on it, if it's likely to break or collapse, hopefully it will do it then and not when you are stood fully on it. He continued, "Ok, fully turn round so you are facing outwards with both feet on the parapet, don't let go of the ladder!" I wasn't bloody going to, I thought to myself! So, there I was now looking down on the little people stood looking up at me, at least eighty foot down. "Step back with your left leg onto the step." A wooden step had been placed on the floor, so the distance down was manageable. "Again, stamp on the step before you put both feet and all your weight on it," he continued. "Same again for the last step," he said. "Follow me," he said, walking over to the other side of the tower, beckoning me to follow. "Stand feet against the wall facing outwards. "He stood right next to me and grabbed at the collar of my tunic. "I want you to lean right over the edge with your arms outstretched like a bird, do not attempt to hold on with your hands," he stated. I started to lean over, and he ably assisted me with his hand on my tunic to get me in a position where from my waist upwards I was hanging right over the edge staring straight down at the ground all those feet below. He then started general chitchat with me.

"Feeling ok?" he asked.

"Yes," I replied – not the truth obviously, but not as bad as I thought I would be. Maybe this sudden confronting of my fear was working.

"No dizziness, quite happy to stay in this position?" he asked.

"Yes, no problem," I replied. My voice maybe an octave higher than usual. So, this is why it was taking so long after each person climbed off before the radio message to ask for the next, I realised.

"What's your name?" he asked.

"Firefighter Cooke," I replied. "Ok, Cooke, off you go back down via the internal ladders." So off I went, climbing back down, pleased with myself at what I had achieved. But my heart was beating a lot faster than normal. Another day over with and back to a home readying itself for the festivities of the New Year.

The questions came, how had the day gone? So, I regaled most of the day's events. I could see when I retold the turntable ladder part that Janine clearly looked relieved that I had done so well regarding the height. She obviously knew that heights were not my favourite thing. When most people were at home in holiday mode, sat there eating and drinking in the warmth, back I was for yet another day of something new the following day.

My brother and his wife, now realising how stressful I was finding this time, were full of encouragement for both me and Janine, that I could do this, and we would both get through it.

Today: hose running and basic pump drills. The training school had a selection of fire service vehicles and fire appliances all parked up neatly side by side in a long engine house. Each squad would be allotted its own fire engine that it would use, maintain and clean throughout the length of the course. Each squad would be attached to one Subo instructor who would also stay with you as well. At this point none of that had happened. It was an instructor and an appliance out on the drill square. I had seen hose running on my visit to my local fire station, but today it would be line up with your hose, run it out as fast as you could and then roll it back up again. This sounds simple and easy. But most of us were to find out, running, holding it out at arm's length without it completely unravelling at your feet was more of an art. Tripping you up, struggling to roll it back up again neatly and it not looking like a complete 'Bunch of Baskets' was a lot harder than it looked. As you can imagine the drill square was full of colourful language from our instructors as to the standard of our hose running. Language and phrases shouted at us collectively and individually that today, would not be politically correct or acceptable, nor allowed. Discipline was dished out with harsher consequences, more colourful language but was done with the intentions of producing a well-trained service. Times have changed dramatically in The Fire Service but at that time it saw itself as the forces did, one based around discipline. It remains that way now, it has to be, the nature of the job demands it. The difference today is much of the military style has long gone. Plus, for many years it attracted those who had served in the forces who wanted to have that structure but to be able to have a full home life. On my course there were ex-forces, Navy, Army, Marines. Even a former police officer as well as a plethora of other jobs and a humble insurance salesman.

But back to the hose running. The fire service had a book full of set drills that it called 'Pump and Ladder Drills'. These drills went back many years and if you were to ask a firefighter twenty years previously about pump and ladder drills, they would have been very familiar with them. Apart from a couple of pieces of equipment which were no longer used, like wheeled escapes and hook ladders (Google them!).

All the pump and ladders drills were done by numbers and set commands. So, you would start off by lining up like soldiers on parade, stood at ease. The instructor would then bellow out the instructions for the particular drill he wanted us to do. For example: "Working from a pressure fed supply I want a line of two lengths into the pump followed by a line of three lengths out ending with a branch working at four bars pressure!"

Therefore, stood in line if he wanted four persons to perform the drill he would then shout, "In squads of four number". If eight people were lined up, we would shout loudly from right, our right that is, to left, "One! Two! Three! Four! One! Two! Three! Four!" The instructor would then ask crew's number, and the first number one would shout "one", the second "two". It didn't end there; I hope you are all following? That was just the start of the performance. "Number one crew," he would shout. "Line up at the rear of the appliance facing it." Then: "Number one crew fall in." At that point Number two would take one step backwards whilst the other three turned to their right, jogging towards the rear of the appliance, number two then following along in their footsteps. Three paces from the rear of the appliance behind each other coming to a halt at attention. You would all turn at the same time to your right. At that point the instructor could say, "Drill as detailed get to work", or if he felt in the mood, he could command us to mount the appliance and start the drill from there. Each point on the appliance had a number. N°1 the front passenger seat where the officer in charge would sit, hence N°1. N°2 the driver who was always the pump operator. N°3 and N°4 in the rear and if it was a five-person drill N°5 in the back in the middle. All this before anything had even been done. Lost the will to live yet? As you can imagine at this early stage, you guessed it, confusion reigned. I think at this point it would have been easier to teach us all the foxtrot.

Finally, this short, sharp introduction into the Fire Service came to an end and home for a few days to celebrate the coming New Year. A new year which would bring the start of our training properly.

We had had our 'canapé' and were now about to start the meal properly, so to speak. Most of us though at this point felt slightly 'shell shocked'.

In the life of a firefighter, when 'the bells go down' that is every time we are called out to an incident. It is at that point when the alerters sound that the real buzz, the knowledge that we never know what we have been called out to attend, begins.

Not long into the start of my adventures on station, one lunchtime just as Cook had called us to the mess room – this took place at 12.30pm and we were expected to have changed into our undress uniform complete with shirt and tie. These were times where life was a little bit more formal. If you were designated as the 'orderly' for the shift, it was expected that you assisted the station cook in her duties and served the meals to the seated watch. This consisted of a three-course meal usually starting with soup. We had already had tea and toast at 10.00am prior to usually going out for 'drill' which could be on station or anywhere in the station area dependent on what we were practising. So, everyone was sat at the long mess table. Station Officer, Subo and Leading Firefighters part of our, at that time, 12-strong team. Firefighters down in seniority to me at the end, the probationer on the watch, sat there not saying 'boo to a goose' and as the soup was being served the 'bells went down'.

Up we all sprang and raced to the Watch Room where the Station Officer tore the printer sheet off and shouted, "Two pumps, kitchen fire". We climbed onto our designated places aboard each fire appliance. Today I was on the first pump, the water ladder, wearing Breathing Apparatus, with another young firefighter who had just completed his probationary period of two years. As we pulled up outside of the rear of the terraced property, we could see smoke pouring out of the broken kitchen window. "Start-up you two," the Station Officer said, pointing at us both. A hose reel was being pulled off the fire appliance by another colleague as we pulled our masks on, ready to enter. At that point a neighbour came shouting that the occupants were at work, but she had seen the son go past down the street about 15 minutes ago. I tried the door handle to find it was unlocked, so we were able to enter without breaking the door.

We entered into what we assumed was the kitchen to find a small orange glow in the corner of the room, just visible through the thick black smoke. Edging nearer I gave it a quick blast with the hose reel spray. It hissed and splattered but after a few blasts the glow disappeared, so we knew it was out. Quickly searching for the windows to open to try and clear some of the smoke, we heard the voice of our Station Officer come blasting from the doorway. "You Ok in there?"

"Yes," I replied, "I think it was a pan on fire, but it's out now."

"Ok," he replied. "Get yourselves upstairs, check there is nobody there and vent," he shouted.

Me and my partner Sam patted the walls in the smoke looking to find the stairs. "I've found the stairs," Sam shouted.

"OK," I replied, pulling the hose reel in so that we could proceed up.

Climbing the staircase again with no visibility, we got to the top to find a door closed.

"Can you hear that?" Sam questioned me.

"Hear what?" I replied.

"That!" he repeated. I couldn't really hear properly apart from the sound of myself pulling on air in my breathing apparatus. "There's something behind the door, it sounds like a monkey."

"A what?" I questioned.

"A bloody monkey," Sam shouted back. "Get on the radio and ask if the owners have a pet monkey inside?"

"Are you sure?" I replied hesitantly.

"There's definitely something that sounds like it's squealing and squeaking behind this door!"

"Team Alpha One," I called over the radio.

"Go ahead" came the reply.

"Does the owner have… a pet…a monkey?" I said hesitantly.

"Please repeat?" came the reply.

"Does the owner have a pet monkey?" again I repeated.

There was a long silence.

Then came the sound of our Station Officer over the radio: "Never mind a bloody monkey, get those windows open and the rooms searched!"

Sam could clearly hear our Station Officer's response over my radio. "I'm going to open the door but just be ready if something jumps out," Sam said next. I was knelt behind him now very wary as to what may suddenly appear out at me through the smoky darkness. Sam slowly opened the door then reached out in the direction of where this sound was coming from.

"Got it!" Sam shouted. "It's bloody wriggling all over the place," his voice getting higher in pitch and the sound of his breaths suddenly getting heavier. "I've grabbed it tightly, it's definitely a monkey."

"Ok," I replied, thinking this has turned into a monkey rescue. "Come down the stairs backward, I'll guide you."

So, carrying the said monkey we made our way down and outside to fresh air. There we could see our rescued monkey in all its glory. It was a slightly blackened, bright Ginger Cat. Sam, arms full of ginger moggie, stood there in front of the Station Officer. "So, lad, your monkey looks ever so like a ginger cat to me," he said, ever so sarcastic.

"Sounded like a monkey to me," came the muffled reply through his breathing mask.

The cat at this point had obviously exhausted itself with all its squealing and had also breathed in a lot of smoke. It was now very floppy in Sam's arms. The appliance driver had set up a first aid station as was procedure in case there were any casualties. Oxygen at the ready. Taking the cat from Sam, he laid it on the ground and proceeded to put a child's oxygen mask onto its face. At that point the young lad from the house had arrived to see all the commotion outside of his property and seeing his cat laid out on the floor, being treated, shouted, "Tigger, that's my cat! Is he ok?"

"He's breathing," said the firefighter dealing with him. "But he's taken in a lot of smoke."

Then suddenly Tigger came round to the fact of his situation, squeaked and squealed very loudly, scratched the said rescuer vigorously all over his hands and ran off down the street, leaving a bloodied, very startled rescuer watching.

So, what had started out as a run of the mill job with a young gentleman who had accidently turned on an electric ring on the house cooker, the only problem being that his parents had placed an electric deep fat fryer on top of it which had then caught fire, had turned into what Sam and I would be reminded of over the coming months repeatedly as "The rescue of Tigger the Monkey".

So back to station, and after cleaning and servicing the equipment, a quick wash and brush up and a return to shirt and tie. We sat down to resume our lunch, which at this point was all laid out at our table, soup, main course and pud! Each with a little 'Chinagraph pencil' name written on the edge of our plate that the cook had written before she had gone home.

Raising his mug of tea the Station Officer spoke. "To our two intrepid monkey rescuers sat at the end!" he said, looking at Sam and myself. "A job well done!" he continued with a rapturous round of applause and laughter from the rest of the seated watch.

I looked at Sam.

"Well, it did sound like a monkey," he came back.

10

Fourth of January.

The start of 13 weeks of residential training had begun. It began with not the best of starts. January had decided it would begin with a proper winter. Snow had fallen on the Pennine hills and Monday had started with the majority of the working population sitting or skidding in slow moving traffic. I lived about 20 miles from the Training Centre, with my wife and young child taking me in our one jointly-used car. Although we had set off early and with a panicked stop at a phone box to inform Headquarters I was on my way, I still arrived nearly an hour late. So, with a quick kiss goodbye I ran into the reception.

"I'm on the recruits' course, sorry I'm late!" I apologised. "Can you tell me where to go?" I said in a nervous out of breath voice.

"They're in the Lecture Theatre," the receptionist replied, directing me down the corridor. "You can't miss it."

Off I trot, slowly and hesitantly opening the theatre doors to be greeted by a half-full seated audience and a smart Subo stood at the front next to a table of what looked like sheets and pillows? I walked slowly down the stairs looking for a spot where I could quietly and discreetly sit down. The officer looked directly at me. "So, you've decided to turn up then?" All heads were now looking directly at me and a stealthy entrance was now impossible.

"Sorry, sir!" I said all apologetic.

"I'm a Sub not a Sir!" came his immediate response.

I knew this but maybe nerves and the fact that I was now the centre of attention had got the better of me. I then repeated the mistake. "Sorry, sir, Sub, I mean." Would the room just please swallow me up, I thought.

"It's not difficult, young man!" he said, pointing to the two bars on his shoulder. "Name?" he continued.

"Cooke," I quickly responded.

"OK, FF Cooke, take a seat but come and see me at the end of this lecture?"

"Yes, Sub," I said, quickly sitting down, glad all eyes were now returned to looking at the front. I was right: there were sheets and blankets and pillows on the table next to him. The lecture was how to make and assemble a 'bed pack' properly. Being residential, we slept in dormitories, two squads to each floor. The course wasn't just to train our Brigade, it also included trainee firefighters from Derbyshire, Lincolnshire and a selection from the oil refineries in Scotland.

The Scottish contingent were privately paying so they stayed in the luxury rooms separately from the rest of us. But we all had to make our bed packs up every morning in the exact way the Subo was demonstrating to us. This was two sheets folded separately to reach an inch thick. One pillow on top of the sheets and one underneath adeptly surrounded and wrapped with interlocking blankets all smartly arranged into a rectangle. This was inspected every day and usually found, despite much time spent getting them correct, to be substandard. Regularly we would return to get changed to find sheets and blankets cast far and wide. Thus, forcing us to repeat the whole process. Inspections of every kind were to be the order of the day, every day, for the next 13 weeks. The lecture came to an end, and we were dismissed for morning break, except myself making my way to the front standing to attention in front of the Subo.

"OK, FF Cooke, I want you, before the end of the day, to write a memo to the Chief Fire Officer explaining why you arrived late today and promising that this will not happen again."

"Yes, Sub," I replied.

"If you are late again during the remainder of the course, then you will be put on an Appendix One."

Basically, each firefighter is given three chances of being disciplined before being asked to leave the course, each one called an appendix. So, the first day of my training ended not quite in the way I had expected.

During the first few days of the course, we were to be given a variety of tastes as to the future life of a firefighter. In one we were gathered back into the lecture theatre to watch videos and pictures of scenes of the mayhem of fire, road traffic collisions, chemical incidents etc. These showed death in all its sometime gory details. One film entitled "Great American firefighting mistakes" showed us various films of incidents in which firefighters at incidents with blinkered and tunnel vision, usually ended up either seriously injured and in many cases dead. These videos and pictures of death and injury were to acclimatise us to the reality of our future careers as firefighters. The type of things we may see and have to deal with. Seeing and watching these incidents is, I can assure you, nothing like being there in reality though.

One of my first confrontations with the reality of death was to come fairly early in my career as a firefighter. A type of incident that sadly I was to attend several times throughout my career.

It was again the early hours of the morning and the lights in the station dormitory burst on, quickly followed by the repeated "beeps" over the station tannoy. The cry of "Persons Reported!" came soon after. This again heightened the sense of urgency. Quickly dressing, we climbed on board the rear of the fire engine and the officer in charge thrust the turnout out sheet into the back. "Look it up lads!" he shouted at us. "It's in Starworth village."

We knew that this was a village approximately three miles away, so the drivers could set off in that direction. But this gave us time to find the exact location on the maps and then direct the driver more precisely.

As myself and my breathing apparatus partner got ourselves ready, the firefighter in between us raced through the pages of the map book to find the location. Peering and leaning through to the front of the cab he updated the driver as to the route he needed to take. With little traffic on the road, we raced quickly along the roads, our blue lights reflecting off the wet surface and glass of buildings as we passed them.

Turning off the main road and along the side roads of the village, we were met with a cloud of smoke across the road, obscuring everything in front of us. We drove closer, and emerging from the smoke an arm-waving figure appeared before us. The wind at that point changed direction and the smoke moved away in the other direction, revealing a detached old stone building with thick black smoke issuing out of most of the windows we could see. The figure was of a neighbour who had been awakened by the sound of banging and crackling from the house.

"An elderly lady lives alone in there!" he said, speaking directly to our Station Officer as we all dismounted from the appliance. "I think she's still in there!" he continued, clearly distressed. "She's a bit of a hoarder I think."

Because it was 'persons reported', both of our fire appliances had been turned out and another from the next nearest station, as well as an ambulance and the police.

"Right, lads, two BAs grab a hose reel, and we'll get in through the main door!" ordered the Station Officer.

We quickly un-reeled the hose reel from its drum on the appliance, ready to make entry. The door was locked.

"Grab a key!" shouted the Station Officer to another member of the crew. The key was another name for a large sledgehammer. We stepped to the side as the firefighter got himself into position so as to get the biggest, most efficient swing at the door lock. He swung with a mighty bang, then crack of the door and frame. Managing to open it about a foot – it would go no further – clearly there was something substantial behind, stopping it.

Smoke billowed out of the door and not far behind it was an orange glow. I blasted my hose reel through the gap going from ceiling to floor. This knocked the glow down but causing a lot more steam and smoke to come back through the door.

"Right, we're going to have to find another way in," said our Station Officer.

He stood back, looked at the building, quickly going to its corner. "There's a side door," he said, pointing. The other two BA wearers from the other pump pulled off their hose reel, running it to the side door.

As myself and my partner had already started up with our breathing apparatus, the Station Officer ordered us to then get a ladder up to one of the first-floor windows to make entry and search upstairs for the missing lady. I made the hose reel ready by looping the branch around and in a loose knot, allowing the reel to make a loop that could be hung on my shoulder so as to be able to climb the ladder. The ladder was being quickly removed from the top of the nearest fire appliance by three other firefighters and was slammed into the glass of the window, smashing it and resting nicely to the right side of the window ledge. This again caused large amounts of smoke out and up into the night sky.

Climbing the ladder and reaching the window, I took the branch from my shoulder and used it to break all the remaining glass in the window frame. Bearing in mind the first two feet off the floor were fairly visible, I could see a gap of about eighteen inches and then nothing but books stacked going vertically into the thicker smoke above. I reached in and patting with my hand I could feel the stack going higher and higher the further I reached.

Squeezing over the windowsill, I climbed into the gap and felt along the wall of books, my BA partner following me up the ladder to the window.

"It's full of books," I shouted back at him. "It's stacked floor to ceiling," I continued.

There was just enough of a gap between the stacked books and the wall to work my way along the outside of the room.

My BA partner Sam climbed in through the window after me. "What the fuck!" he shouted at me.

"I know," I replied.

"I'll try and pull enough hose reel into the gap behind me," Sam continued.

I went on following the gap which was now clearer to me as it appeared to be around the outside walls of the bedroom.

The centre completely stacked from floor to ceiling with books and boxes. There was no fire in this room and the smoke got a bit lighter to the point where I could see about a foot in front of me through the haze. At that point I reached the door to the bedroom. I felt the door with the back of my hand, and it didn't feel hot. The problem was that I could only open it as far as the gap of stuff would allow me. Which wasn't very far. I yanked at it, pushing it against the pile of things stacked up. I managed to get it open enough to squeeze through the gap but in doing this the little visibility I had disappeared with the influx of smoke from the rest of the house.

"Alpha team two?" came the message over the radio Sam was wearing.

"Alpha team two go ahead," Sam replied.

Whenever Breathing Apparatus is used, a Breathing Apparatus Entry Control is set up with a board. This board has details of wearers, who they are wearing with, how much air they have entered the fire with. With that it can be worked out at what point the wearer's low air whistle will go off. At which point the wearers should be out of the fire. This is all on a tally which the BA Control Officer slots into a board. Their location and what tasks they are following is also written down.

This is all about control and safety, at all times. It is one of the main reasons the UK Fire Service has thankfully a low death rate. The tally connects to the firefighter's automatic distress signal unit. This is a motion detector, so if a firefighter doesn't move after a short period this starts to sound very loudly. It can also be pressed manually at any point to signal for help. This device can only be switched off once the firefighter collects their tally from the entry control office and plugs it back into their own ADSU. You may see firefighters who are wearing breathing sets do the firefighter shoulder wiggle. If they are not moving, a pre warning signal goes off and to stop the full sound going off which then cannot be stopped except with the key at the BA board, they will wiggle their shoulders from side to side.

Many firefighters around the world do not operate in this same controlled manner with set breathing apparatus procedures and as such pay the consequences.

"Alpha Team Two, can you give a location and gauge check over" came the voice of the entry control officer.

I looked at my gauge which when held up to my face mask I could read the luminous dials. "120 Bar," I shouted at Sam. "Team Alpha Two, one two zero and one ten bar, our location is still the first-floor bedroom. The room is full of junk, over."

"Message received, over" came the response.

"Sam, I'm going to squeeze through the door, it's really tight," I said, pushing myself through the gap. With relief there was space on the other side, the landing was relatively clear. Visibility was still nil and it suddenly became a lot hotter. I crouched down and felt the wall on my right and then the left – this was clearly a corridor. Pulling more hose reel behind us so we could continue further, hot blasts of steam billowed around us from behind. We both crouched nearer to the floor for cooler air, realising that at that point on the lower floor water must be hitting the fire and blasting steam upstairs to where we were.

"You Ok, Sam?" I asked.

"Yes, it's getting a bit warm on the old lugs" came his reply.

We continued along the corridor until we reached another door, which was closed. Checking it again before pushing it open, it went so far and then hit something behind it. I put my weight against it and it moved forward a bit more. In the smoke as we entered, we could feel it was cluttered with stuff but not like the previous room.

Clattering and clambering over things, trying to make our way through the room, searching and feeling as we went. I reached and then felt a window.

"Sam, I've found a window, can you radio and let them know I want to smash it and vent."

"OK," Sam replied. Sam passed the message and permission back to go ahead.

I swung the hose reel branch which is metal at the window, breaking it. I could hear it shattering on the floor outside. I quickly cleared the glass away around the edges, smoke billowed outside and the room soon became visible. Through the smoke as it cleared gradually, I could see a bed with a very blackened figure on top, arms outstretched reaching towards the other window in the room. Her head was back, mouth wide open and eyes wide open but clearly with the relaxed look of death on her face. She had obviously awoken, which is unusual as smoke normally acts as an anaesthetic. We were later to find out that she had mobility issues so maybe the noise of fire in its early stages had awoken her before the smoke had become too much and stopped her attempts to get to the window for help. This was also in the days before smoke detectors were commonplace. It was also clear that to get her out now the quickest and easiest way would be the window. It was clear at that point with the chatter over the radios that the fire was confined to downstairs, but that access had been just as difficult for the other teams to get in, extinguish the fire and try to gain access upstairs. The whole house was just a storage place for boxes, junk everywhere with a network of passageways you could just get through which the lady had used to go around the house. The room we were in with the poor old lady cleared of smoke, and we had passed an urgent message that we had found a casualty. Within seconds the face of our gaffer appeared at the window we had broken.

"Right lads what's the situation?" he questioned. At the same time he was questioning, his gaze fell upon the poor lady laid on the bed. It was evident that there wasn't much hope for her but that was not our job to decide. Ours was to rescue and make every attempt to resuscitate and try. "Right, I'm going to get the paramedics straight up here!" he quickly replied. Obviously making the decision if there was a chance to resuscitate it would be better started as quickly as possible here in the room which had now cleared of smoke and with the fire under control.

"Get the paramedics up here!" he shouted down, himself now climbing in through the window to be with us. The ambulance crew quickly climbed up, passing their bags in to us.

"How's your air?" questioned our gaffer, quickly checking our gauges which were getting very close to our whistles going off. It didn't take long for the ambulance crew to make the decision that resuscitation would be pointless, and that the lady had been dead for a while. This meant that this had now become a crime scene, and everything would have to be kept exactly as it was, including the casualty for the police and coroner to investigate.

"Go, shut down and change your sets," the Gaffer said. We quickly decided that the easiest way was to go out via the window rather than struggle retracing our steps through the labyrinth.

12

So, my first real confrontation with death in a fire situation. One that would be repeated many times over the next thirty years. Hoarding is a problem that is more common than you would imagine. I was to attend into double figures incidents that involved hoarding to the extreme over my firefighting career. Most of which would lead to either serious injury, but sadly more often death. This hoarding would be of the most unusual things. Papers, magazines, bottles of urine, junk of many descriptions? One even had a bedroom full of ladies' knickers, each with the gusset with a neatly cut hole! I will expand no further on that one.

Mental health issues can affect people's thinking in a variety of ways. Ironically, the final fire death I was to attend at the end of my career was again an elderly hoarder. It was an extremely sad but also a slightly delicate situation.

We were called out this time in the middle of the day. Again, it came as persons reported.

On arrival, smoke was issuing from downstairs with neighbours again outside to inform us on the situation. This was that it was an elderly man who lived alone and was thought to still be inside. I was partnered that day with my crew commander (previously known as a leading firefighter). We broke in, clambering over piles of rubbish, books and furniture. Through the smoke in the front room, we could see the glow of the fire. This was rapidly extinguished, and I quickly found a window. Radioing for positive pressure fans to be switched on, I broke the window to vent. This showing how firefighting techniques had changed over the thirty years, but more of that later. Two powerful fans were placed outside the front door forcing massive amounts of clean fresh air into the property. This had two immediate effects. Firstly, hot gases which could cause one of the firefighters' greatest nightmares, a "back draught", to be greatly reduced. Secondly to quickly get smoke through the vent point and outside. The change in visibility was almost instantaneous, allowing us to see the door to upstairs and therefore to quickly continue our search. The stairs once again had been reduced to a small passageway with the right-hand side piled high with books.

We reached the bedroom, opening the window to clear the room of smoke. Immediately we could see an elderly gentleman lying on his back on the bed, trousers down by his ankles. He was clearly unresponsive. We grabbed him to carry him outside as quickly as possible. At the bottom of the stairs, we met another BA crew who had arrived from our next nearest station. (At that time our once two pumps and turntable ladder after twenty years of cutbacks had now been reduced to one pump and five firefighters on the crew. That again is another story!)

"Can you pull his pants up?" I said to one of the crew members. He pulled the gent's pants up, covering his modesty so we could take him outside with as much dignity from the viewing public. It was not uncommon for us to wait for an ambulance in the modern emergency service world. They are under the same budget cutbacks and are stretched far beyond what they should be. Training in our Brigade in casualty care and Intermediate Trauma Life Support had been at the forefront of our Brigade's training for the preceding 20 years. One that I had been keen to follow and adopt. We now carried and were trained in the use of trauma packs, airway management, resuscitation, defibrillation, spinal immobilisation, pain and burn management, gunshot wounds and even childbirth. The last two, again, I kid you not, but then again that's another story.

A casualty care area had been set up ready outside of the property to receive the rescued gentleman. We laid him down for the awaiting firefighters who would quickly assess him and would start to try and resuscitate. That allowed myself and my partner to drop our sets and catch some fresh air. We watched on as the firefighters started chest compressions, put an airway down his throat and attached defibrillator pads on his chest to see if there was a shockable rhythm. "Do not touch patient analysing rhythm" came the digital voice of the Automated External Defibrillator. Both firefighters who were attempting resuscitation sat back on their knees as the machine did its checks for a rhythm in the heart it could shock. "Continue CPR" came its next digital response. The firefighters immediately started chest compressions and assisting breathing with a bag, valve and mask over the casualty's nose and mouth. I looked at my BA partner and he raised his eyebrows in response. He didn't have to say anything but we both knew that this wasn't a good sign. The paramedic in a car and a double crewed ambulance then arrived and our guys gave a quick casualty handover to the paramedics, continuing CPR as they went. The paramedics connected their more advanced equipment to see what was going on with his heart. A joint effort then got him into the ambulance, which was a better environment to continue. We went back into the property to retrace our steps and see the situation in a clear environment. We got into the front room, which was a complete clutter of furniture and things. There was one chair in the corner that you could sit on. The carpet that was visible around the chair was covered in burn marks and spent matches. A rack of smoking pipes on a shelf next to the chair. The chair was completely burnt, and radiating around it so was everything else. The fire had then gone up the curtains and along the ceiling.

We continued upstairs and could hear our Gaffer moving around in the bedroom we had found the poor old gentleman in.

"Have you seen this, lads?" he questioned us, pointing to the bedside table. We both looked and on top was a very large bottle of hand pumped hand cream. Next to it stacked high was a very large selection of pornographic magazines.

My BA partner looked at me, laughed and then stated. "Well, that explains why his pants were down by his ankles then."

Some may find that an insensitive thing to say, considering the situation that someone had just lost their life in a tragic event. But humour is one of many ways to vent feelings and deal with images of extreme situations. They have to be dealt with one way or another. If not, they build and build and can lead to problems with mental health issues in the long term. Mental health is an open subject today, thankfully. This wasn't always the situation though. You were expected that these things are part of the job so just "Man Up".

There is an element as well of being slightly detached mentally from the situation you are in. Yes, you can be part of a traumatic incident, and scary and difficult things can be happening around and to you. But the training and the experience gained as you go along, allow you to function fully and do what is needed.

Speaking of training, back to training school...

13

The 13 weeks of residential training were very regimented, and every part of the day was run in the same way as a school with our own set timetable. We were expected to be up and out of bed by 7.00am, bed packs neatly made.

Each squad took it in turns to be on what was called "picket duty". This meant that the squad on picket duty had to be up even earlier, march out on the parade ground and raise the Brigade flag up the very tall flagpole and then stand to attention, salute the flag and march back in again; the flag was raised before everyone was up. This was then repeated at the end of the day at 10.30pm. This was the time everyone had to be back at the training centre, signed back in. The squad had to remain in full uniform for the day and couldn't have their two allotted pints of beer from the training school bar. Which incidentally had its very own friendly bar steward.

If we weren't at the local swimming pool first thing in the morning or out for a five-mile run before breakfast, breakfast would be at 8.00am. Full English breakfast, tea, toast and cereal, provided by the then on-site catering team. Then it would be straight outside, lined up in squads to be marched round to the parade ground where we would be inspected in our Dexys Midnight Runners working rig. This, even though it was just a bib and brace denim outfit, still had to be neatly ironed with a nice crease running down each leg. Shoes cleaned and buffed up with toes you could see your face in. Stood to attention whilst an officer walked in front of us pointing out each bit of fluff and crease. "Not good enough, get that sorted" would come the comment, usually from a senior officer who had more hairs and fluff on his uniform than all of us put together.

Parts of the day would be practical drills, pump and ladder drills on the drill square, the drills getting progressively more and more complicated. Pump drills with more lines running up ladders and lines into buildings. Ladders put up in varying manners, confined spaces, down passages and then turned into the building from right angles. The parade ground a cacophony of sounds. Each squad with their own fire appliance and instructor. Each squad separately following their own particular drills. Shouts of command emanating from every direction.

Practical Drill sessions were alternated with lessons. There was an incredible number of different things to learn. We had to learn about every piece of equipment from how the pumps and primers worked right down to a simple stirrup pump, each part broken down, how all these pieces of equipment were tested and how often.

Practical firemanship, building construction, knots and lines, again not just how to tie them but every type of material used to make them.

Hydraulics which included formulas to work things out like ‹jet reaction› $R = 0.157\ Pd^2$ ‹Nozzle Discharge›. L-3312 WP. In the fire service there are endless mnemonics to remember lists of things. Properties of this thing and properties of that. The amount of learning just seemed to go on and on. To add to the pressure, practical and written tests occurred regularly. The thing was you were expected to pass everything. So, plenty of the evenings were taken up with our heads in books and reading our notes.

There were lighter times as well. Times in the pubs nearby and in the city near to the training centre. Times where comradeship was established and friendships that would last nearly four decades later. Always back by 10.30pm though, safely signed into the register kept in the entrance.

Because there was so much learning, occasionally our squad instructor would give us the nod. "We are going to learn about the properties needed to create a good vacuum, this might be worth remembering," he might say, looking at us with raised eyebrows.

This was a time where the importance of the fire service going out into the community to educate regarding fire safety was becoming the forefront of its priorities. We were told that once we were on station it would be expected of us that we would carry this out by visiting homes, inviting groups to the station and one very important one, that of visiting schools and giving school talks about the work of the fire service and the importance of fire safety. One such visit in the very early days of my career would stand out.

14

You may remember that years ago the Fire Service had its own mascot. " Welephant." This was an elephant dressed up as a firefighter. If Welephant was needed for duty, a courier would deliver the full suit to be worn by the lucky volunteer. This volunteer, if we can call them that, was usually the newest member of the watch. Yes, the lucky probationer would be the one to have to put this large outfit on with its large, helmeted head and long trunk. We had been booked to attend one of the local primary schools.

Leading us into the main hall today's lucky probationer donned his outfit clearly very reluctantly prior to entering. It was clear that Welephant wasn't too happy. His body language said it all. We all walked into the school hall to a very excited and noisy audience sat cross legged on the floor. Seeing Welephant, the cheers became even louder.

Welephant gave them a wave and then stood at the front. The Station Officer then went on to give them a short talk on fire safety and not phoning the fire service when they weren't needed and the consequences of making hoax calls, a big problem at this time.

"Now Welephant is going to show you how we as firefighters search a room which is full of smoke and we can't see," said the

Station Officer. "Welephant, go around the outside of the hall and show the children the BA Shuffle."

Welephant reluctantly started his manoeuvre, arm or should I say foot, going up and down in front of him and one leg sweeping the floor in front of him, looking for any obstacles. "Welephant is using his arm, children, to feel if there is anything in front of him," explained the Station Officer.

"There might be things like electric wires in front of him – that wouldn't be very good, would it?" he questioned the young audience. "You can see him shuffling his foot in front of him – what do you think he is doing that for?"

All hands went up in the air across the room. Pointing at one of the children, the Station Officer asked. "Yes, what do you think?"

The child hesitated and then said, "Is he dancing?"

A few of the children chuckled at this answer.

"No, he's not dancing," he replied. "If he's using his hand to check in front of him for what he can't see, what's his foot doing?"

The little girl put her hand back up along with the others. The Station Officer pointed back at the little girl, taking the risk that she had now got the correct answer.

"Is he checking what he might walk into, like a hole?" she came back in reply.

"Spot on," said the Station Officer. "Yes, there might be an obstacle in front of him and like you say a hole he might fall down."

Welephant at this point had made his way right round the outside of the hall and got back to the front where we were all stood with the headteacher. The Station Officer raised his hands in front of him, gesticulating. "Now, children, Welephant is going to do a little dance for you," he said, pointing in Welephant's direction.

The muffled answer came back from inside the suit. "No, he fucking isn't!"

The Station Officer stood there aghast. We just looked in the direction of the headteacher; she then came forward to the front standing next to the Station Officer who was still speechless.

"I think Welephant is feeling a little tired, children. He's been very busy, hasn't he?" she questioned, looking to see any reaction from the children sat at the front.

"Let's give him a nice round of applause to say thank you for coming today."

As the children cheered and clapped, Welephant made his escape outside. Needless to say, when we got back to station the gaffer pointed at him. "My office now."

Welephant was to make a name for himself on another occasion too, this time with another probationer inside.

The town had an annual Gala Day. This was a day where a procession of floats, groups and bands marched right through the town centre. It was a big event where most of the town turned out to line the streets and watch.

The fire service was always asked to attend, and we used the situation to walk by the sides of the fire appliances with buckets, collecting money for the firefighter's charity or as it was known then The Fire Service Benevolent Fund. Our appliances were always at the back of the procession so if we got a fire call, we could peel off quickly and attend.

So, it was decided the turntable ladder would take the lead and, sat on the ladder at the front, Welephant could then wave at the crowds. The two fire engines could follow on behind. We got to the assembly point, Welephant got dressed, climbed onto the ladder and made his way to the front of the vehicle where the ladder came to an end above the cab. At this part of the ladder, it is where a monitor is plugged in and when the ladder is extended a firefighter can direct it, firing the water jet with a long handle. The monitor was not plugged in, but the handle was a permanent part. Welephant sat down, legs astride the handle to make himself comfortable for the ride.

We set off on the parade to large cheers, people pointing at Welephant and lots of laughs and giggles from the passing crowd. This continued all the way through the town. Lots of money was being thrown into our buckets and we thought what a very successful day.

The following week the town newspaper came out and as usual a large centre spread of photos of the event. And there large as life was a big, coloured photo of Welephant waving, with the handle between his legs looking like he was sat with a very large erection. The reason for the town's amusement was now very apparent.

15

Training continued at its relentless pace, both physically and mentally.

Contact with home was via the training centre's phone booth. Twice a week, off I would toddle, coins in hand to feed the hungry beast its endless appetite for ten pence pieces. This short time was to catch up and make sure that everything was going OK at home. To tell each other how much we were missing each other. Also, for many weeks, to offload the numerous areas I was struggling with.

One particular week things hadn't gone particularly well and I started to really doubt that I had made the right decision in joining the fire service.

"I'll back you up whatever you decide, but don't make any rash decisions" came the advice over the phone.

Phil, the retained firefighter who I mentioned earlier was in my squad, he could see I was struggling with things. We had many talks together. "Look, Mark, life on station is not like life here," he would say. "They're pushing your buttons; they want to see a negative reaction."

Not knowing what station life was going to be like, all I could see was a very blinkered view of the present situation.

"Bite your lip, put up with the shit, it's only three months of your life," he would say, many times. "Play the game", "or treat it like a game". He was right. These moments would come and go with the varying pressures put on us. As well as this, the times when it was a struggle there were just as many good times if not looking back a lot more. Times of comradeship, laughter, and real fun. We would get together on an evening in the training school bar for our so-called two pints. Or we would frequent the two local pubs who loved it when a course was on, especially if it was a large one. Many a laugh was had regarding things that had happened in the day. Taking the piss and pulling each other's leg was all part of how we coped and gelled with each other. This was how it would be on station when that far off time would eventually arrive. Yes, some of these friendships would last till today, the far distant future.

16

One highlight of the week though was always Friday. Friday was always a day of inspections and cleaning.

Usually there would be a march around to the drill square in either full fire kit or full undress uniform. This took place in all weather conditions, and mine being a winter course it was usually freezing cold or raining, and on quite a few occasions snow.

There we would stand at ease until the training school Commander would make his appearance. The command to come to attention then would be bellowed out. I think he would look out of his office window, see us all standing there, and go and make himself a cup of tea. Twenty, 30 minutes sometimes, we would be stood there, at his command. He would then process down the lines now stood at attention, picking bits of fluff or a hair he had found. "Not good enough, lad," you would hear down the line.

On one particular week it was a purge on hair length. "You're not a bloody seventies pop star," he would say to someone stood with a very tidy short back and sides. "I can nearly stand on that, lad," he continued his quips as he walked along. Then it was announced that the following Monday a hairdresser would be available in the evening to cut hair. This as it turned out was a serving firefighter who arrived with a set off shears, offering one style: short. I think his only training had been with sheep. A coincidence you might ask. Not sure how much commission the Station Commander was on.

Then in the afternoon the fire appliances would be stripped of all equipment, and everything would be cleaned and polished. Later in the afternoon another inspection would take place in our dormitories. Everything was expected to be cleaned and polished. Bed packs neatly made. Dorm cleaned and tidied. This also included toilets, showers and the cleaning room. Once this was completed, we would stand at the ends of our bed at attention. The Subo would then walk up and down the dorm, throw the odd bed pack on the floor. "Again, lad, this time properly" would come the command to the unlucky one. It was a lottery as to who would be chosen as they were all completely identical.

One particular Subo had a slight speech impediment in which he struggled pronouncing his t's. In he would storm, usually finding something obscure.

This time his hand held up high in the air. "What's this? What's this?" He gesticulated as if he was about to announce that a murder had been committed in the toilets and he had found the murder weapon. "A pube, a pube?" came the announcement. "I've found a lickle pube in the shower?" He stood there with his find held between finger and thumb. The pressure not to burst out laughing was almost unbearable, especially the way he pronounced "lickle pube".

On another occasion it was fluff. Again came the announcement with the evidence held aloft. "What's this, what's this?" Then holding it six inches in front of the face of the nearest firefighter. "I've found fluff in the dryer, fluff in the dryer." He seemed to need to repeat everything twice as if we hadn't understood the first time. "What are you all, animals?" continued his indignation.

Each week whilst this was going on, I would keep an eye out, repeatedly turning around when the Subo was carrying out his inspection. Looking out through the window for the arrival of a mega bright yellow car parked on the main road outside of the main gates. I could see this vehicle clearly from my window. Its arrival meant Janine had arrived with my little girl, ready to go home.

Incidentally, when I went to buy this car, the only condition my wife had given me was don't buy a yellow one. It was such a good deal though and as it turned out very easy to spot its arrival.

Knowing all our eagerness to go home, the inspections were usually dragged out and prolonged on purpose.

When we were dismissed, out we would all run like children at the end of a school day. I can still see and feel the sheer joy of opening the rear door of the car to see the happy beaming face of my little girl in her car seat. A kiss from both of them. "Aaah" – the weekend had started, sheer joy.

All too quickly though, Sunday afternoon and evening would arrive. If the forecast or weather was bad, I would make the reluctant decision to go in on the Sunday evening, not wanting to risk the threat of a discipline for repeating my first day's mistake.

Thankfully, arrangements were in place as the guys from Scotland were there, as they only went home, I think, once a month via a plane flight. Also, those from other counties on the course would usually also arrive Sunday.

After a kiss goodbye, in I would walk with that sinking feeling in my stomach ready for another week. At least it gave me time to iron my working rig and bull up my shoes for the morning inspection, or if an exam was coming, time to revise. Come Monday and the arrival of everyone else and straight into it, there wasn't much time to dwell on things, we would be too busy.

17

Halfway through the 13-weeks course, we would concentrate totally on firefighting and the use of breathing apparatus. This was a time where we would be actually fighting real fires in the smoke house.

The smoke house was a large concrete structure filled with many rooms, corridors, stairways, raking ladders, hatchways and tunnels. These could be configured to represent various types of building. The rooms had metal cribs that could be filled with wood and set on fire to simulate a real fire. The walls were built to withstand the heat that would build up inside and that would give us an understanding of how fire behaves and the signs to look out for when dealing with it. Dummies filled with sand could be placed around these rooms for us to find in the smoke, and rescue.

Scenario after scenario would be set up, each one different. All starting with the same safety briefing and questions. "Is everyone fit and well to take part?" would come the question. "Watches and rings removed or taped up" it would continue.

Oxygen and a first aid station would be set up ready. If a situation did occur, then a full evacuation signal would be given of repeated whistle blows. As well as the use of the extractor fans being put on to clear the smoke and heat as quickly as possible.

Then would come, "The runners and riders will be…".

This was the instructions as to what everyone's role would be in the exercise. Whether you would be pump operating or wearing breathing apparatus and what team you would be, or if you were to be running breathing apparatus control outside. The larger the exercise, the more of each would be needed. Sometimes it would be entry from the ground floor and work our way upwards. Sometimes it would be to put ladders up to the roof and make our way down through the building.

Now we were being subject to real fires, if you were wearing breathing apparatus it was very hot and could be extremely exhausting dragging 12 stone dead weight casualties out of the building by various means. This would give me my first experience with the heat of a fire, the confusion and sometimes complete disorientation that can occur. But this was always in a relatively well controlled environment. Sometimes things would go completely tits up so to speak. In the debrief which always followed each exercise, we could get some real bollockings. "If that was a real fire, this team would be dead" came the exhortation from the sub-officer taking the debrief on one exercise, pointing at the map of the scenario projected on the wall. "You became completely blinkered by the situation," he continued.

On this occasion the team of four had found two casualties and attempted to rescue both between them. What they had failed to do was work out the fact that they had used half their air in searching and getting to the casualties. Two of the team members' low air warning whistles had started sounding long before they had reached the exit. This was a real safety "no-no". As the Subo pointed out they were so blinkered and focussed on getting their casualties out, they had compromised their own safety.

"Who was entry control officer?" came the next question from the Subo taking the debrief. I raised my hand awaiting my fate. "You should have been on top of the situation, Firefighter Cooke," he said, directly looking at me. "Did you not ask for them to give you gauge readings?" came his next question.

"Yes, Sub," I replied, "two had just used over half of their air just before radioing to say that they had found two casualties."

"Did that not alert you in any way?" came his next question. "Did you not think they will struggle to get out before their whistles went off?"

"I wasn't sure," I replied.

"Well, that's not being in control, Firefighter Cooke, is it?" he came back.

I could now feel the whole room looking at me. "Your job as entry control is to oversee the situation, to keep tabs on where the teams are and how much air they've used and to make sure they are out before any whistle sounds," his voice getting sterner. "If this was a real situation and someone had died, a crime scene would occur, your breathing apparatus board would have been impounded, and you, Firefighter Cooke, would have ended up in a Coroners Court explaining yourself," he concluded.

Lesson learnt.

Control in a fire situation was taught repeatedly with each exercise we went through. In reality, it was even more important as lives and the safety of others was critical. It is also why the UK Fire Service has one of the best safety records and, also thankfully, a very low number of firefighter deaths on duty.

This is fine when everything goes to plan. But with fire you are dealing with so many unknowns and rapid changes in circumstances.

18

During my future career I was to go to countless numbers of mill fires. Yorkshire's industrial past was built on textiles. Mills becoming larger and larger and more numerous as the boom in textiles grew ever greater and greater.

Some of these mills were massive complex buildings. Multi-storey stone-built structures that would eat up an ever-growing workforce. As time went on the processes producing floor after floor of oil-soaked wood. Yes, a fire waiting to happen.

In the early days of my career many were still in production but the writing on the wall could be seen by us all. As time was to move on, so economics were to change and so many fell into disrepair and lay idly empty or change of use entirely.

One of the very first large fires I was to attend was to one of these buildings.

By coincidence and the strangeness sometimes of life, at the end of my career I was also going to attend one of the largest mill fires in the country. It would happen a matter of weeks before I was to retire. This also would see those controls being tested to nearly disastrous consequences. But that's for another time; back to this first time.

The bells this time went just as we had finished our morning routines of toilet and shower cleaning, mopping the engine house after washing all the vehicles, whether they needed it or not. General tidying up all round.

We were just about to take our seats for breakfast after the tannoy went with the announcement "tea and toast ready", when the repetitive "beep, beep, beep" sound of the turnout went off.

The pre-determined attendance at this building and also the fact that smoke had been reported meant that we had what we called a "Circus turnout". That was when all vehicles at the station, two pumps and the turntable ladder were called out at the same time. When this happened, it was quite a sight. The engine doors all being cast open and the three vehicles exiting the building, blue lights on and sirens sounding. When this occurred a set order had to be followed so as to stop an accident where one of the vehicles could cross another's path. So, the water ladder with the Station Officer on always went first, followed by the water tender, then at the rear the turntable ladder. Usually, each vehicle chose a different siren type so as to distinguish to the driving public the noise of each vehicle and as they passed would realise that a different vehicle was also going to pass next.

The call had come in via control from a young chap who had gone to investigate after his mother had smelled smoke. The lad's dad had worked at the mill and when he saw the smoke, he knew that it was coming from the basement. The mill wasn't very far from the station and as we got nearer, we were met by the familiar pall of smoke crossing the road in front of us. There on the other side of the road stood a lady with a young lad at her side.

"Second pump get into a hydrant!" went the order from our Station Officer over the hand-held radio.

"Right boss," came the immediate response.

"TL crew stand by 'till I find out what's going on," came the next order from the boss.

We knew the mill well, it was one that we used for drills, etc.

The boss dismounted and spoke to the mum and her son who confirmed what he suspected, the fire was in the basement of one section of the mill that backed onto the river that ran alongside.

Nobody was at the mill at this time of the morning, but the owners and key holders were contacted immediately by control as soon as the call had come in. The mill was a range of three, four and five storey buildings arranged in a rectangle with access through to the central courtyard via a huge stone arched entrance. The boss jumped back on the pump.

"Drive through into the courtyard," he ordered the driver. "Water tender run the water from the mains through to use in the courtyard," he said via the handheld radio.

We drove through into the courtyard which was clear of smoke but would give us access into the building. Pulling up, we all dismounted and made our way to the main door into the section that was on fire. There weren't any visible signs of the fire on this side of the building.

"Right, lads, we'll have to break in," said the boss.

One of the lads went straight back to the pump, and opened a locker, grabbing a door breaker. This was a two-person operation as the one we carried at that time was a hefty lump of metal that operated like a medieval battering ram, held by a person on each side, swinging it backwards then hitting the door with a mighty crack. The door swung open inwards, hanging off one hinge in the opposite direction it was meant to open. This opened into a long corridor down which at the end we could see smoke making its way towards us. There wasn't any heat at this point.

At this stage the leading firefighter from the other pump arrived with another firefighter. "What do you want, boss?" he asked.

"We need to find the source of the fire," he replied.

"TL crew, can you get to the river side and see what's going on?" he again radioed to the crew outside.

"Roger" came the reply.

The boss, looking at the leading firefighter, then spoke, "Can you get a BA team of four and start laying a hose line down into this corridor and see if we can locate this fire's source." Pointing at me and the two stood next to me: "Get kitted up; Sam, can you get entry control set up," he said then looking in Sam's direction.

We all quickly ran back to the pump to grab our BAs and gather together where Sam was setting up the control board. The leading firefighter, Keith, once we were all together then spoke: "Right I'll take the lead." Knowing that two of us were still in our probationary period, me only a matter of a couple of months, he pointed at me and Pete the other probationer. "You two, behind me and stick like glue; John, can you take up the rear." A probationer sandwich so to speak. He then continued to quickly brief us. "We're going to run a hose line dry as far as we can get, any sign of fire I'll give the order to charge it over the radio."

Other firefighters at this point arrived with us from the next nearest stations that had been called out. The Station Officer had quickly radioed the other pump to send an immediate assistance message to make pumps eight for water and BA crews.

A couple of firefighters started to run hose on the outside of the building. It was flaked backwards and forwards on the ground ready so we could make our way into the entrance and down the corridor to the smoke front.

"Everyone ready?" asked Keith. A couple of us were just finishing dressing, rearranging our gloves or fastening our helmet straps. "Yes," came the communal response through our masks.

"Sam, radio check, over," he asked to Sam who had set the entry control board up near to the door.

"Loud and clear, over," Sam responded.

In we went following Keith the leading firefighter who picked up the branch connected to the hose laid on the floor. Each of us in the team picked up the hose and stood at each other's back and made our way down the corridor. Reaching the smoke, Keith turned to us and speaking loudly through his mask so we could all hear, said: "Stick to the left-hand side, we'll follow the wall and see how far we can get."

A few paces and that was it: no visibility. There was just the sound of four firefighters feeling their way in the darkness, shuffling our feet on the floor, each waving our free hand in front of us to see with our hands what was around us. The repeated foot from the chap behind catching you up with his swinging foot. We carried on for maybe 20 more feet.

"I've reached a door," said Keith. "I'm just going to feel if it's hot," he continued. This he would do by taking off his glove and with the back of his hand feel the door top to bottom for any heat. This we would do with any door, but it was even more important at this time as the hose wasn't charged with water. "It's not hot," he said. He pulled the door open. "I'm going to wedge it open."

Keith was a very experienced firefighter with about 15 years' service at that time. Not many firefighters kept a few little wooden wedges in their pocket for this very purpose. But that's experience gathered for you.

Further on we went, pulling the hose behind us. The room we had now entered sounded completely different; everything was more echoey. The feeling was of space.

"Alpha team one, are you receiving, over," came the familiar voice of Sam on the radio.

"Go ahead, over," went our reply.

"Can you give me a gauge check, over" came Sam's reply.

We all held our luminous gauges up to our visors so we could see them, each of us giving our readings verbally so they could be radioed back. Sam would then write them down on his board and using the lowest reading work out roughly when we should be out.

We carried on, the room now getting hotter the further we went but there was no visible sign of fire. No faint glow through the smoke. Following the wall and reaching a corner we then turned to the right, the heat always staying to our right-hand side. Another 20 feet or so and another corner to the room. The heat now seemed to suddenly ramp up.

Keith stopped in front of me. Then after a moment spoke. "Everyone, I want you to stop breathing for a moment so I can listen."

We all held our breath to stop the sound of our breathing apparatus and listened. We could hear crackling and banging but it was muffled. Then the sudden sound of us all breathing again.

"Stay here," Keith ordered us. "I'm going to feel out into the floor." We could hear him shuffling out into the floor.

"Right, we need to get out bloody quickly, the fire's underneath us and the floor's bouncing a few feet out" came Keith's sudden announcement.

We all about turned to retrace our steps. "Speed it up, lads, the fire could break through that floor any second." All our breathing rates got faster and the heat just seemed to suddenly go through the roof, causing us to crouch and try and get a bit cooler air. Keith quickly radioed back to Sam that the fire was on the floor below us and we were coming out. We were all breathing so hard now that Sam couldn't hear the message through the noise. Keith had to repeat it.

We got to the exit, the heat and smoke now following us out. It was clear at that point the fire had broken through the floor in the large room we were in.

We all went to Sam at the board, grabbed our tallies and each started to shut down our sets.

Keith, his mask now removed, looked at us. "That was bloody close" he said. "If we'd stayed in that room any longer, we'd all be bloody toast now." Again, looking at us all. "I don't think you realise how close we were."

I just thought if it wasn't for being with Keith and his experience how different things may have turned out. Every so often Keith would just make the comment in passing, "We were bloody close, Mark," and I knew exactly what he was talking about. Especially on a watch night out after a few drinks. This was not the end of our work here to get this fire under control and eventually out. The result: to save this historic building.

It was at this time that thermal imaging cameras were being introduced into the brigade. The aim was that each fire appliance would have its own. These were handheld devices about the size and shape of the old video cameras when they first came out. We had thermal imagery at this point, but they were on specialist vehicles and about the size and shape of a brandy barrel.

Ours hadn't arrived at the time of this fire. But when it did a few weeks later all our thoughts were the same. If we had had one what a difference it would have made in seeing the heat build-up in that room. Thankfully now these are readily available to all firefighters and with the advancement of technology so much smaller and more accurate. A lifesaving piece of kit.

The fire in the mill had made its way from what we now found out was a lower basement underneath the room from which we had had our narrow escape. It had gone through the floor and was now trying to spread outwards and upwards by any means it could. An entrance to the basement had been found down a stone cobbled walkway in the corner of the yard. Plans were made for breathing apparatus teams to make their way in and fight the fire at its core here and to also hit it from above. It was also now a priority to make steps so that the rest of the building could be protected. As you can imagine, this would take a lot of firefighters and equipment. Time was also a priority.

Now that more resources had arrived, it meant that two or three teams could advance their way into the building with a charged hose. This, as always, turned out to be more difficult than was first thought. Once the first teams had made their way in, they were met with a labyrinth of tunnels all jam-packed with wicker baskets on rollers, all filled with wooden bobbins. These were obviously leftovers from the mill's heyday.

Not only were they difficult to move and get around and through but were obviously the fuel feeding the fire further into the basement. Several crews now had battled their way into the basement and had eventually found the fire front. The problem was the basement was a labyrinth, a rabbit warren of tunnels. What made it worse was there was no way of fighting the fire from outside. The only way to fight it was to hit it from the floor above where we were at the point it had broken through. Or via the tunnels, one part at a time. Empty air cylinders were now piling up outside in the area the BA crews were now using to set up and to service their sets after use.

A selection of senior officers, or "White Helmets" as we called them, had now arrived to take over command. Twelve pumps and the turntable ladder were now in attendance. Also, the command unit had arrived to house the white helmets and organise the whole affair.

Jets and ladders were set up to form a stop so that the fire couldn't hopefully spread to other parts of the mill complex. We had been tasked to put one of the ladders up so a jet could be put on part of the roof section. I was grabbed on the shoulder by a passing officer. "Grab a set," he said to me, then pointing at two of the guys stood next to me: "you two as well, we are going to need you to wear in the basement," he said to all three of us.

«We›ve already worn," said one of my colleagues.

"Looks like you're wearing again" came his quick response.

So off we trudged to grab the sets we had serviced and put back on the pumps. Once we had got our sets we went to the officer where teams of wearers were gathering. As we got nearer to him, he said, "Can you go to Bravo board and get instructions from them–" he pointed over the courtyard near to the slope where the entrance to the basement was.

Because there were so many teams now wearing BA sets to fight the fire, three different boards were now set up to keep track and control the wearers. Alpha, Bravo and Charley. Each team would be given a designated name. We were the fourth team to be set up at Bravo board so our call sign would be team bravo four. Hoses had been run out all over the place, it was covered so the whole area looked like a bowl of giant red spaghetti had been spilt.

We were given our briefing from the entry control officer. "Follow this line in," he said, pointing to one of three hoses that were snaked outside and into the doors to the basement. "Bravo team two are on their way out," he continued, pointing at a map drawn on the back of the BA board scribbled in Chinagraph pencil. "It looks like if you make your way along this corridor, you'll reach another going left to right at right angles to this," he explained. "There are a series of passages each full of stuff going off this long corridor, the fire is down a series of these?" He pointed at the drawing and these passages were going off this corridor like the spikes on a comb. "The problem is you'll have to go down them one at a time, that's why it's taking so long." This information had been gained from previous crews and the knowledge of the caretaker who had now arrived with keys to access all parts of the mill.

We handed our tallies in as a crew, each one checked by the entry control officer that our air pressure matched our gauges, and our time of entry was written on each tally. Following the line in it led us into the start of the basement. Visibility wasn't too bad, but it was an obstacle course that had to be tackled all the way in. Previous crews had pushed wicker trolleys full of bobbins etc out of the way to make any kind of path further into the basement. About 30 metres in visibility got worse with a mixture of smoke and steam from the water from the jets further in. It was very humid, causing us again to stoop lower to get to cooler air. Then we could hear the sound of other BA wearers and voices ahead. It was the other team on their way out. Sensing our presence, the voice came through the dark. "Team on our way-out, guys," came the voice.

"We're here to take over what you were doing," I replied.

Through the cacophony of the sound of heavy breathing we managed to have a brief conversation. "Follow the line down this passage till it turns left, we've put everything out down the right-hand side," the voice instructed. "The hose we've pulled back, it's a bit looped but you'll find the branch on the floor."

"Cheers," I replied.

In all situations the outgoing team has priority so we all just stood where we were and grabbing each team member passed them along the line like a human passes the parcel. Once they were all passed, we continued on our way following their instructions. The heat now was getting pretty uncomfortable and the sound of the fire crackling and banging away very evident.

"I hope we get this branch soon," I said, verbalising the thought running through my mind, the security of having water to fight the fire with now a priority. We soon found the looped hose and followed it through our hands in the darkness until we could continue further along. As the guy had said, soon after the branch was on the floor. A thought of relief as I picked it up. "Stick to this wall on our left and we'll follow it along the corridor," I said. Being at the front with the branch meant the others had to follow my lead. They would have to drag the hose behind me from the loops on the floor. Making our way on, the flickering glow of the fire became more evident through the smoke and steam. The cobbled floor was getting deeper with pools of water from the jets onto the fire. Opening the branch, the jet reaction pushed me back onto my crouched legs; thankfully, the next guy pushed his shoulder into my back, stopping me from going arse over tit. I was obviously hitting the fire as a plume of steam and the hissing of the water shot our way down the corridor.

We kept on crouched down on our haunches, moving the jet around, trying to get every area of the fire covered. Then over the radio the voice of the entry control officer asking for an update and could we do a gauge check. "Roger that," my colleague replied. A quick check of each of our gauges and the information was passed back.

"Keep an eye on your gauge readings, you've only got ten minutes to your time of whistle" came back the voice of entry control.

Hearing that, I spoke to the rest of the team. "Right, let's give it a good blast for five minutes and get out of here."

"OK" came the response back from the others.

The five minutes soon went, and we turned on our heels and made our way out, sloshing through the ever-increasing pools of water on the floor.

On our exit and return to entry control, we gave a quick recount of what we had done and the situation we had left. A white helmet who was stood nearby came over and spoke to us. "The tea wagon has arrived outside the mill on the road – go service your sets and grab a brew."

He didn't have to ask twice so off we trotted. The problem was after you cooled down everything that was wet with sweat had now become cold and uncomfortable. So here we sat with our brew and a ready-made "pot noodle". Our brigade wasn't renowned at that time for its provision of substantial refreshments. We looked in envy at the other Emergency Services that had proper canteens with real food.

At one protracted incident in a neighbouring brigade, the senior officer of that brigade turned up and ordered a guy in a van to go to the nearest well known and renowned fish and chip shop and order 60 portions of fish and chips, giving the firefighter carrying out this task his own credit card.

Back to the pot noodle, normally at a going job relief are ordered via control after roughly four hours. Resources being brought in from surrounding areas to allow those who have been working hard to have a rest. This didn't seem to be happening at this incident for some unknown reason. We had been there nearly four hours now and there was no sign of being relieved yet. So, pot noodle now consumed, off we went as a crew to find our officer in charge and see what was going on and what we were to do next.

The fire ground was still a hive of activity but the fire in the section we had been in looked far more in control now and the smoke a lot less black and billowing, coming out a lot whiter now.

We found our Station Officer stood with several other white helmets, a common sight on any fire ground. He looked at us, seeing how wet and bedraggled we looked. "Been working hard, lads?" he said with not a hint of sarcasm. A reply of grunts and groans was his response.

"I've been round to the control wagon to see when we can get relieved, but there's another large incident in the brigade and control are struggling with resources," he continued. "It looks like we could be here for a while."

And a while it was, long enough to be called to wear breathing apparatus for a third time. Back I went this time as a team of two. But interestingly we were tasked to follow the same route as our close call earlier in the day. The fire at this point had been knocked back to hitting the hot spots. As we were tasked from control, we were given one of the new thermal imaging cameras and instructed to follow the hose line to the branch at the end and direct the water to the hot spots we could see through the thermal imager. Sets donned, off we went, reaching the branch on the floor where we looked around through the camera's screen, looking at what we could see. It was evident that most of the floor had burnt through from the basement below, now leaving a massive void down to the floor below – this confirming our lucky escape a few hours earlier.

A close call indeed.

19

The intense Breathing Apparatus training period on the course eventually came to an end. After lots of simulated fire incidents covering every type of scenario you could think of – house fires, basement fires, tunnel fires, high rise, garage fires, searching off guidelines and branch lines safely using the personal line attached to each BA set – you name it, it was covered to try and make it second nature.

Heat and humidity training was one of the final delights. This was meant to show us the dangers of both heat exhaustion and heat stroke. Both very serious but extremely deadly. This training was stopped shortly after our course as health and safety rules deemed it as too dangerous. A room in the smoke house was set up very hot but also very humid with a very high moisture content in the air. In this room was a set of wooden stairs going up and down. Each person went in wearing BA and told to pick up two containers full of water one for each hand and then to continually walk round the room in circles, going up and down the stairs. As you can imagine it didn't take very long for this to become exhausting and for your body temperature to go sky high. The instructor repeatedly asking you questions to see your mental response – heat exhaustion can cause complete confusion to the person it affects and if your core temperature gets to a certain level as stated earlier it can result in death with heat stroke.

Around I went.

"You OK, Firefighter Cooke?" asked the instructor.

"Yes, Sub," I replied, continuing on. After ten minutes of this I was soaked, starting to feel weak, the water containers feeling like lead weights. I was also starting to feel very lightheaded.

"What's your home address?" came his next question.

"Erm," I said hesitantly as though he had asked me to recite the whole of one of Shakespeare's plays. "Five er, five Rowan," I repeated hesitantly.

"Right, firefighter Cooke, get out, strip down, get some fluids in you and cool off quickly," he quickly responded, guiding me to the exit. "Just remember this feeling in the future – you never want to experience this in a fire situation." Exiting the door to the awaiting audience. "Right get your set off and fire kit, there's water to drink," he said, pointing to a stack of water bottles on the floor. "There's also a hose if you need to cool off and O_2 if you need it," he continued, pointing to a resuscitator also on the floor with an O_2 mask connected.

20

Then as one last treat for us they filled the complete smoke house with high expansion foam. This was used in things like ship fires or installations where water wasn't the ideal thing, either for its reaction or damage. It basically smothered the fire. A guideline had been laid in one end, up and down stairs, through rooms and out of the other end. We were tasked to follow this line each in contact with the person in front by one hand on their shoulder. A long conga line. Once inside, visibility was nil. But the really weird thing was sound was muffled so the only thing you could hear was your breathing and the sound of your heart beating. To communicate with the person in front or behind you, meant getting head-to-head and shouting very loudly. If you had any form of claustrophobia this would freak you out.

You don't realise how much we rely on sound for spatial awareness. So off we all went snaking our way through, feeling with our feet and free hand attached to the guideline. An automated distress signal unit from a BA set had been hung on the wall, continually sounding. But you could only hear it when you were a couple of feet away from it. You couldn't even hear the other BA wearers breathing, only the sound of yourself. When I burst out of the doorway the sound of the world around hit you as well as the light. Very rarely do we experience absolute darkness. I hoped I never had to use this in anger and thankfully I never have.

21

My course starting at Christmas for 13 weeks hit the worst months, for bad, cold weather. At one point I inevitably succumbed to a winter bug. Aspirin taken, I went to bed early to try and sleep through it. I had a temperature and felt lousy. I eventually got off to sleep and was dead to the world. Bad timing – tonight the instructors that stayed over had decided that it was cold enough to carry out a full fire drill and evacuation. We had been told that in the event of the fire alarm going off we were to immediately exit the building and parade outside so that a roll call could be carried out. This was the early hours of the morning and off the bells went with a constant ringing. I awoke to Phil who slept in the bed next to me, half-dressed, shaking me vigorously. "Mark, get up!" he shouted, shaking me on the shoulder. "Get up, it's the fire alarm," he continued.

At that point I had no idea where I was – for one moment I thought I was in my bed at home and my wife's voice had gone all weird and why had she put the lights on!

"Get dressed, Mark," Phil instructed.

I sat up, seeing figures running past the end of my bed, quickly making their exits. The dorms were on three different floors, and a few were staying in houses that were on the training school grounds. I got up, putting my clothes on as Phil, now dressed, made his exit.

Still slightly disorientated and feeling lousy, I made my way down the stairs and into the freezing cold outside. Once outside, running as we were required, to my position in the parade line up. There I stood in the semi-darkness and freezing cold, shivering. Not knowing whether from my temperature, the cold or a mixture of both. Others arrived and then stopped suddenly, with several gaps of where somebody should be stood now still empty. We stood at ease, with one instructor facing us, equally looking perplexed as to why. People had stopped arriving. I stood there thinking if this is what it's like getting up and out in the middle of the night to a fire call, it was something I really wasn't looking forward to. The fire alarm stopped sounding and the instructor with us spoke.

"Right, stay here, you lot, I'm going to see what's going on," he ordered and off he went back to the main entrance. At this point I really didn't want to be here. I just wanted to be back in bed, nice and warm and fast asleep. Soon after the instructor came back out. "There's been a bit of an incident; can you make your way back to your dorms," he informed us.

We went back in and there on the ground floor near to the bottom of the stairs was a group of fellow missing firefighters and instructors gathered around one sole gent on the floor, looking very much in pain. One of the guys from one of the other brigades had made his escape that fast he had fallen down the stairs and had clearly broken his ankle. This was sad for a couple of reasons: one, this would be the end of this course for him, and he would have to start again at the beginning once he had recovered; and two, he would not finish and pass out with us – having spent two-thirds of the course in our company.

Physical fitness throughout the course was taken as top priority. Twice a week before breakfast we would set off in the brigade coach to the nearest swimming baths, rolling back the thermal cover so we could have a swim. It was taken for granted that you could swim when you joined, but some people were better than others. The aim was that you would pass your gold swimming and lifesaving badge by the end of the course. Breakfast back at the training school after this early morning excursion would be a hearty full English. Gym work was also carried out regularly with fitness testing to assess improvement. One instructor informed us that we would never be fitter than when we left this course. We all ate heartily three good meals a day as well as toast and cakes at break times. I lost a full stone over the time of the course and had muscles like Popeye by the end. This was on top of the fitness regime I had followed prior to the course to try and get myself physically ready.

The brigade had provided us top notch gear to carry out our PT; this included black plimsolls. Yes, no expense spared for us recruits. These weren't too bad in the gym, but for everything else, including the regular five mile run off site, were an absolute nightmare. It's a wonder there weren't more injuries. Another physical delight they had for us was to split us into teams of six, each having a telegraph pole that we were required to carry and run with around the training school grounds, up and down the hills with it on our right shoulder then our left, or held straight up above our heads. One day some bright star decided it would be a great idea to do it wearing full fire kit and our breathing apparatus sets. All this at what sometimes seemed like a beasting was taken without any real questions as to why. It was seen as the best way to improve fitness, working as a team and to create the best recruits ready as they can be for the job ahead.

One day a football match was organised. This was nearly at the end of the course, between the officers and instructors. As you can imagine, pride was at stake – neither side wanted to lose. For some reason the football used was a thing that looked like it had been made in the 1940s. A great big brown lump of leather. The ref on numerous occasions had to calm the game down as both sides seemed to be prepared to go at it with no holds barred. Part way through, the ball was kicked hard towards me and I decided that it was a perfect opportunity to head it towards the goal. Bang, instead of hitting my forehead I got the angle wrong and it slammed right into the top of my head. I literally saw stars for a moment. I was stunned. I managed to finish the game, but my head was bouncing. I think we lost but I literally cannot remember. I mentioned to one of the subs that my head really hurt. He said go see the brigade nurse and let her have a look at you. Off I popped to one of the houses that was used by the nurse and doctor when he was there. In I went and explained what had happened. She checked my eyes and vision.

"I think you may have a touch of concussion," she informed me. "I'll give you some paracetamol and you need to take it easy for a couple of days."

"Right," I replied.

"If you get any dizziness or sickness you need to inform the instructors immediately and see us straight away," she said quite sternly.

"Yes, no problem," again I replied.

"If you want, I can put you on light duties for a few days to recover?" she then questioned.

But this was the last thing I wanted. A couple of people on the course had been put on light duties for various reasons and length of time. But this meant catching up on training lost or the possibility of being back squadded.

"No, no thanks," I quickly replied. "I'll be absolutely fine." Now wanting to get out as quickly as possible.

"OK, but like I said, any changes you need to inform us" came her quick response.

Out I went with a headache that lasted several days but I was still on the course. Paracetamol would be my friend for the next few days.

Road traffic accident training was next, or as it is now referred to, road traffic collision training. This was a great respite from the hectic days of breathing apparatus training. Most of the week was spent at a nearby scrapyard where we were given the opportunity of learning to use the various pieces of equipment and later in the week to put that to practice with live casualties in numerous scenarios. At this point in time a transformation in equipment being used was just starting to take place. On most fire engines in our brigade, a limited amount of rescue gear was carried on each one. Some of it had been in use for decades such as the Senga saw and the Senga reciprocating cutter. Both of these were powered by compressed air, which was provided by a couple of BA cylinders. Very basic by today's standards. We had also hand operated hydraulic equipment. What most people know as the 'Jaws of life' were carried on emergency tenders with other advanced gear. This thankfully was to change over the next few years. As fire safety was to become a priority in the home with home fire safety checks and the mass take up of smoke detectors, the number of rescues from deaths in house fires and domestic properties would slowly decrease, but with a correspondingly large increase in the number of rescues from vehicle accidents. All first appliances throughout the brigade would become heavy rescue pumps. This meant that these appliances would end up carrying hydraulic cutting gear, hydraulic rams, electric saws. High- and low-pressure air lifting mats, chocks and blocks for vehicle stabilisation. Protection for casualties, tear drops and sheets that could completely cover casualties and carers in the car or vehicle whilst rescue was taking place. Casualty care training alongside this would be advanced massively. Appliances and crews would be trained in more advanced trauma care and life support. Defibrillators would come into use with bag valve and mask resuscitation and airway management. Trauma packs would be carried with everything needed to provide care, including burn shield, long boards and collars to provide spinal immobilisation, Entonox gas to give pain relief. It was a massive change that would take place over the coming years. Alongside this, over the same period, would be a great change in the technology of vehicles, providing greater safety but also greater challenges for firefighters dealing with these vehicles.

Together with our changes, changes in the ambulance service would also take place, with the provision of more paramedics on ambulances that were able to provide more and more advanced care.

On the RTA week, one of the key focuses was one that was called the 'Golden hour'. This was seen as crucial. The golden hour was basically the time from when the accident took place to the point where advanced life support was able to be given to the casualty. This was the point in time when the casualty arrived at Accident and Emergency. The chances of the casualty surviving or making a better recovery from their injuries was greatly increased if this was achieved. With the advances that were to come over time with paramedics and advanced paramedics or even doctors on scene now, and the back-up of the fire service, it has meant that the golden hour has been extended so to speak, advanced treatment being given on scene or before transportation.

Back in the scrapyard we continued having great fun cutting up cars. Practising the removal of casualties from vehicles in every position you could think of. On their roofs, on their sides. Even with casualties with false wounds and blood.

The big thing though was that it wasn't reality, these were not real people with real life-threatening injuries. They weren't scared or in distress. Family members were not dead or seriously injured sitting next to them. There were no sounds of people in real pain. There were no children screaming or crying in panic. There were no people with broken or missing limbs. Nobody was questioning you that they were going to die. No blood or vomit everywhere.

Yes, we were shown lots of videos and photos of distressing scenes, but that doesn't prepare you properly. The reality is very, very different. And it was one I would soon experience. One that would be repeated many, many times in numerous different scenarios over the coming years.

Road Traffic collisions as you can imagine can happen anywhere and everywhere on our road system. Each one is different in its causes and outcome. Vehicles have changed dramatically over the last few decades. Advances in safety and technology have brought greater survival rates. Turning up to incidents that 20, 30 years ago you would have said the casualties would have been very severely injured or dead, now people can be out and walking around. But with the increase in traffic and car ownership it has meant that more casualties are rescued in road traffic incidents now than that in a fire situation. Again, in the early months of my time on station, the reality of dealing with collisions other than that of a training situation would become apparent.

The early hours of the morning on another cold winter's day, the bells went down, thrusting us out of our lovely warm pits into the cold of the night.

"Person trapped on the bypass" came the call from the first person to pull off the paper from the printer. "Police on scene," he continued.

Both pumps from our station were called and also from the town the bypass went to. They would make their way on one side of the dual carriageway, us on the other.

Arriving along the road, the blue lights of the police car on scene shone out like a lighthouse beacon. As we got nearer, we could see what the situation was. A car had lost control, skidded off the road sideways and collided with one of the streetlamps. These were not the usual streetlamps – being on a dual carriageway they were the sixty-foot-tall steel ones. Travelling on our side of the carriageway we would obviously be the first crews on scene. The pump from the other station would have to travel to the next junction to come and assist us. We got off the pump, the OIC going to the police officer to assess the situation. A couple of colleagues and I got off and did the first thing we always did at an RTC, that is to get a hose reel off and run to the vehicle ready in case of a sudden outbreak of fire.

As we dragged the reel to the car, the sudden sound of my colleague in front of me falling flat on his arse could be heard. "Fucking watch that!" came his announcement. "It's black ice!" he continued, informing us sat on his backside.

It was clear from this that the car had hit this sheet of black ice that ran up the road and lost control. What now became suddenly evident to us was the extent of the damage. The lamp post was flat on the floor with the front and rear of the car wrapped around it. It was also at an angle partly down the slope at the side of the road.

"Right, can we get this vehicle secured and get access to the driver and see how he is" came the order from the gaffer. "And get some light on the situation," he continued.

A clatter of pump locker doors and equipment being retrieved could be heard now in the normally peaceful time of night along with the sound of the vehicles lined up, engines ticking over, exhausts churning clouds of vapour in the cold, looking more like they were running on steam. The first thing was to stabilise the car so that it was safe to work in and around, and also to keep the casualty's movement to a minimum.

"Whoa!" came the exclamation of another person to find the black ice. "Watch that everyone" came his sagely advice.

The gaffer was now radioing to the pump operator to get in contact with control to see if we could get a gritter wagon here to sort this ice out. Thankfully, there was little to no traffic on the road at this time. I then heard the police officer on scene shout to our boss that he had got the bypass closed to traffic from the previous roundabout.

One of the firefighters that had made access through the window to the driver, enabling him to assess him, turned around and looked at me. "Grab the O_2 and first aid kit."

"No prob," I responded, quickly turning on my heels back to the pump to get them. As I got back to him, I could see the firefighter manually holding the guy's head in what we called the 'neutral position'. This was the head looking straight forward with the chin at right angle to his shoulders. This would keep his 'c' spine in one neutral position to minimise damage to his spinal cord and also keep his airway open.

"I've got the gear, Andy," I said to him.

"Set the O_2 up," he instructed.

I looked into the vehicle, curious as to the situation.

"He's breathing, but he's totally unresponsive," Andy continued.

At this point an ambulance had not yet arrived. As I looked in, I could see this poor chap completely scrunched up in a gap no more than 18 inches wide, from the door to gear stick in the middle. The steering wheel nearly at his chest. His legs had been thrust upwards by the dashboard and there in full view was an open wound – his left femur snapped in two with the bone sticking out so that you could see the bone marrow. Surprisingly there was very little blood. The gaffer came over to get an update.

"This is going to be tricky," he said not surprisingly. "I think we'd better get out Hunter One." Hunter One was the call sign of the vehicle based at our nearby hospital. This was a Land Rover equipped with various medical equipment and a doctor or nurse or paramedic from the Hospital's A and E. An arrangement had been made that if we or an ambulance attended an incident that needed more expertise at the scene, we could radio for Hunter One to attend. This arrangement would remain for several years until budget changes and an increase in the training of ambulance personnel to paramedic status, as well as I have previously stated a dramatic increase in our equipment and training in dealing with trauma-related incidents over the coming years. Today we have the marvellous work done by the Yorkshire Air Ambulance. What is still surprising is that this is a charity, totally funded by the general public's generosity. Long may it continue.

The OIC got straight onto his hand-held radio to the driver of the pump. "Can you send a priority assistance message asking for Hunter One to attend, over."

"Roger that" came the immediate response.

The gaffer and the Subo in charge of the second pump then got together with the other OIC from the neighbouring station that had now arrived. Although I couldn't hear exactly what they were saying, I deduced by the gesticulating and pointing they were coming up with some sort of plan of action to get this poor chap out. Then he called all of us that at that point were not tasked with a job.

"Ok, set up an equipment dump over there," he said, pointing at a flat piece of ground by the side of the road. "First job, we need to remove the whole of the roof. Once we've done that, let's see if we can get the door off the driver's side and get access to his lower limbs and see if he's trapped or injured further down?" he continued, being met by several nodding heads. "It's looking like we may have to use two Tirfors front and back to pull the car apart and hopefully relieve the pressure and give us access." He looked around at his attentive audience.

By this time the first ambulance crew arrived and had made their way to the speaking OIC. "OK, let's get to work," he ordered, turning then to the ambulance crew to update them as to the situation.

The Subo then pointed to three of us. "You get on with setting up the gear to get the roof off–" and then pointing at those remaining. "You lot get the Tirfors set up, and try and get attached around the wheel axle front and back driver's side," he continued.

Orders given, off we all went to get the gear off the pumps.

"You grab the genny, Cookie, and set it up on the road away from the car" came the order to me by one of the senior firefighters.

As I grabbed my lumbering piece of equipment, the others grabbed theirs, running the coiled up hydraulic hose along the ground towards the car which now had the ambulance crew there making their assessment of the casualty. Two sets of hose were run out from the generator so that on the end, the cutters could be attached to one and the spreaders to the other. The cutters were basically a giant pair of scissors that could cut through metal very easily. The spreaders can obviously spread metal things open but can also crush metal in its jaws. This equipment you may know as the jaws of life.

We were now set, ready to systematically cut the roof off.

"Can I have a quick go and see if I can pop this door open?" said one of the guys to the nearby station officer.

"Yes, give it a go" came his quick response. "Are you ok with that?" he asked the ambulance guy monitoring the casualty.

"Yes, no probs," he replied.

Another firefighter was leaning in now through the back window, hands either side of the casualty's head, maintaining that neutral position. The guy was still obviously unresponsive but maintaining his breathing. Deep groans could be heard coming from him every so often. We were taught at training school that if we attended an incident and people were screaming, crying or hysterical, it usually meant they were OK. Firstly, they obviously had an open airway and were breathing normally. It was the quiet ones to be immediately concerned with. If their response to voice, pain or indeed not responding to anything, then something serious was happening medically. The chap with the jaws pushed them into the gap between the door and body of the car, slowly using them to make a gap. The metal on the door bent back then the jaws popped out of the gap, jolting the car slightly and making a loud bang. Little movement is always crucial, so this was not ideal. He closed the jaws shut again and pushed them further into the gap he had made. The point where he had pushed them in was right where the door latch was. The aim was to spread and break this point. The door creaked and groaned, the metal around the lock tearing away. Feeling and seeing what he was doing, he gave everyone a warning: "It's going to go," then with a similar bang as before the door sprang open, held by an awaiting firefighter. He pulled it back, at which point the OIC instructed, "Get the door off, cut the hinges". Another firefighter holding the cutters then stepped in to cut them, allowing the door to be completely removed.

Now it became apparent how scrunched up the casualty was. The whole of the engine had been pushed sideways and into the passenger compartment. This had forced his legs upward, his body pinned by his seat and the dashboard and steering column. This had snapped his left femur, and now looking at it, his right lower leg and ankle, both of which were pinned now by the pedals. He was almost in the foetal position.

We continued to cut the posts of the car, sawing through the bottom of the front windscreen so the whole roof could be lifted off in one piece.

Hunter One had arrived, the doctor and his assistant now making their own assessment of the situation. The roof was off and you could see the laboured breath of the casualty in the cold air. For that matter, everyone's morning breath steamed out, looking like a smoking room.

The Tirfors were now being set up as well. This piece of equipment was a manual hand winch with a steel cable that ran through. It could be used to either drag a heavy object along the ground or be used to lift an object vertically.

The doctors and our OIC grouped together to finalise their plan of action. With any type of crush injury to any part of the body, if the casualty has been in that position for more than ten minutes great care needs to be given. Toxins build up in the trapped muscles. If these are suddenly released into the bloodstream, it can cause sudden Cardiac Arrest. The doctors wanted to get the patient cannulated so that drugs could be quickly given if needed and intravenous drip set up to give fluids. As I said previously, amazingly there wasn't a lot of blood. The body can do wonderful things in times of trauma. Shutting things down not needed at that time, like blood to your extremities, and allowing it to concentrate where it is needed the most – your vital organs and the blood supply to your brain. The other concern the doctor had was that we at that point had no idea whether his position was hiding any major blood vessel damage. Any release could give cause to a sudden catastrophic bleed.

I watched as the doctor put the cannula into the patient's lower arm. The doctor's hands visibly shook. The thought went through my mind that even experienced trained personnel when confronted with such traumatic situations can feel nerves, or maybe it was the cold, or a bit of both.

The doctor and ambulance crew now ready, signalled our next step in the proceedings. "Gents, we need to try and pull evenly with both Tirfors and at the same pace" came the directions of our OIC. "On my command," he directed. "Pull."

Both Tirfor operators winched slowly the long handle that operated the winches. The screech and crunching sounds of the car could be heard, then the sudden shout of the doctor, "Stop!"

The OIC immediately shouted "Rest!" – the fire service order to stop the task you are involved in, although both had stopped as soon as the doctor had shouted.

"The steering wheel is going downwards as you are pulling," said the doctor, turning to inform the OIC.

You could quickly see the OIC contemplating the situation for a moment. He then pointed to the firefighters stood back that were not tasked with a job and the chap who was stood still with the spreaders. "Get the chains attached and set up to pull the steering column back."

Again, a flurry of activity occurred.

The doctor turned to our boss. "I think we need to be quick as we can getting him out, his blood pressure is dropping quickly," he said now with concern in his voice.

"How about we get your stretcher with a spinal board." (Now called a long board so as to not alarm the casualty with the word spinal.)

"If we slide him across sideways, all hands on, and then slowly lay him out straight?" came back the boss's plan.

"OK, let's do that," the doctor responded.

Again, a quick flurry of activity to prepare this scenario. I assisted in getting the stretcher from the ambulance to the side of the car, helped by another two firefighters. As we got nearer to the car, one of the firefighters with me had not yet been close enough to see the casualty. As we started to move him, the dressings that were covering the open wound slid off. They couldn't be attached at that point because of the casualty's position. This would have to be done as and when they could during his move onto the long board. So, the wound was visible again and for the first time for my colleague to see. His eyes opened wide in an obvious look of surprise. He didn't say anything; he didn't need to. We proceeded to carefully manoeuvre this chap into position laid along the long board on top of the awaiting stretcher. A cervical collar had been fitted around his neck to keep it in alignment and also to keep movement to a minimum.

He moaned as we moved him, but there was no real response. The group of breathing, steaming individuals got him into the back of the ambulance to continue his assessment and get him to A and E.

It was always a good feeling at this stage, casualty safely on his way. Now time for us to clear up. Equipment and pieces of vehicle strewn across the floor. As this was a serious RTC and deemed life threatening – the casualty may not recover – it was time for the police to do their thing. Accident investigators would now log and measure the whole scene, marking on the ground any notable marks etc to try to establish as much as possible what had happened. As it was the early hours of the morning, there weren't any witnesses to take statements from.

Chatter of what had taken place, speculation etc was the conversation as we cleared and restored equipment back onto the pumps. The ambulance now on its way in the darkness, its blue lights illuminated the dark, cold winter's night. This wasn't an exceptionally difficult, gory incident. There weren't multiple casualties with extreme injuries. People hadn't been thrown through the vehicle's windscreen. Limbs weren't missing, even heads which I was later to experience. I have recounted it because after all the practice of training school, it was the first reality of seeing and dealing with real people, with a real person with real injuries; and there is a big difference.

25

I make a point as myself and other members of the emergency services who over the time of their careers, 30 years or more, may experience multiple times of seeing and dealing with extreme situations of trauma and stress. As one wise person once said to me, remember it's cumulative, you can cope and it's really not a problem, but there may come a point in the future where it becomes too much and your mind and sometimes your body says enough.

My father-in-law said to me on numerous occasions when I had joined the fire service, oh, you'll be bloody brilliant at snooker. When I mentioned incidents to him, his attitude was, "Well that's what you get paid to do, you wouldn't join the army if you weren't prepared to shoot someone." There were many times in the future when I thought I wish I could put you in my situation, see through my eyes what I'm seeing now, deal with what I'm dealing with, and let me watch your reaction. Again, the TV is now full of programmes following the emergency services. The point I'm trying to make is in your armchair watching on a rectangular box, there is a big difference to being there and it being your reality.

The future would bring road traffic collisions in many shapes and forms, multiple casualties, head-on collisions, people crushed under vehicles, thrown from them. Adults and sadly on occasions children dead at the scene etc, etc. Life extinguished in the blink of an eye. Whether caused by dangerous driving, alcohol and drugs, speeding or simply the unfortunate circumstances of life. Like the gentleman mentioned and described just now, hitting a sheet of black ice in the early hours of the morning returning to his home from work… and if you are wondering, the story does thankfully have a happy ending. After a long hospital stay, the overcoming of serious infection, the surgical pinning of both legs and lots of additional surgery and endless physiotherapy, he did recover. We don't always find out what happens to people – on many occasions when they've gone to hospital that's the last we hear. Except those unfortunate enough that their final journey in life has already started at the scene of the accident. But sometimes we get a visitor on station armed with goodies to just say thank you. Or a card sent through the post. They are always special moments. Like long-lost friends recounting their traumatic situations, we would go through what they remembered. The person usually saying the same thing – "I don't really remember too much." The odd snippet will come or has sometimes remained etched into their memory. Like "I remember a voice saying his name was Pete and everything was going to be OK then he squeezed my hand". That's what happened here: over twelve months later he turned up after making a call to the station secretary to find out who had attended. She did a fine job searching the records to see that it was Blue Watch. Now that's job satisfaction.

26

Training continued apace; subjects changed, others were recapped. Each day was as busy as the next until the arrival of those glorious Friday late afternoons. Practical drill sessions intermixed with lessons in the classroom. On the cold and wet wintery days these lessons would be a welcome respite from the freezing hands and faces of drilling outside. I still do not comprehend the reason behind not giving us gloves to wear. As the course continued nearer to its completion, we would venture out to the local pubs, well to both of them. To let off steam away from watching eyes. These two pubs, over the years had got used to the attendance of the latest recruits. A nice little boost to their incomes. Things never got really rowdy – the threat of a not very happy landlord making a complaint kept things contained, and the fact that if we weren't back and signed into the register by 10.30pm we would be disciplined. The real nights out would, with luck, come very soon, hopefully in celebration of everything passed, ready to pass out at the end of the course. Fire safety was obviously going to be part of the course as it would play a large part of the firefighter's life on station. But Fire Safety Legislations, as you can imagine, is about as interesting as studying any form of legislation – yes, mind numbing. Occupancy numbers, escape distances, required firefighting equipment etc, etc, etc, you get the picture. It does bring to mind though of one lighter incident related to fire safety.

27

It was morning parade on our first day back on duty after our rota days. The usual directives of who was doing what for the day and on which appliance was delivered.

"Just a reminder, everyone, this afternoon we've got a fire safety open day," spoke our then Subo, raising his eyebrows. Character wise, he was a bit of an enigma. One minute he was 'Mr fire service', everything needing to be shipshape and Bristol fashion, done pronto and to the book. On other occasions, I kid you not, there he would be, pipe and slippers. On occasions actually sat in a chair with a large cigar, puffing away, again slippers on feet. Today was a pipe and slippers day.

At that time the Subo would take over command of the watch when the station officer was on leave. We had two Sub-officers on our watch at that time. The other Subo was an absolutely smashing guy, a real gentleman who was coming to the end of his career as a firefighter. A member of 'The Cocoa Club'. Those on the watch who had over 20 years of service completed were eligible to be part of this group, and yes, you've guessed it, partook of the said drink before bed. He too loved a pipe and regularly when the bells went down would turn out puffing away on his pipe. Then when an attendance at an incident would have to do his own firefighting. Banging away on his tunic pocket as the pipe set fire to it.

Our instructions given out, the Subo continued. "Can we make sure everything is set up in the engine house ready for this afternoon?" he instructed. The engine house was set up with tables covered in leaflets regarding various hazards to be found at work and at home. One of the major problems at that time was fires caused by the often then used chip pan. A video was played on loop connected to a television on a stand, showing the dangers of overfilled, unattended chip pans. Also, what to do in the event that one should catch fire. Advice now completely shunned. Instead, the advice now would be to get a deep fat fryer with a thermostat or just use oven chips. The afternoon arrived with a steady stream of people wandering around each station asking questions or stood in front of the TV watching the video. All was going smoothly until one person who was attentively watching the video, shouted. "Excuse me, I think your telly is on fire!" Looking across I could see wisps of smoke coming out of the back of the TV. I went over to switch it off, and one of the other firefighters said, "I'll let the Sub know." The wisps grew darker and thicker as I approached. The Subo was apparently sat in his office, slippers and sunglasses on, reading a book. But on hearing the news burst out of his chair, slippers still on, and ran through into the engine house.

I at this point had grabbed a CO_2 extinguisher and was about to discharge it into the back of the TV. At the same moment another firefighter had opened one of the engine house doors to let the smoke escape. The Subo was having none of it; gesticulating madly, he started shouting. "Evacuate the station! Evacuate the station!" he shouted in a large booming voice.

Although people had stepped back in caution to allow us to put it out, no, the Subo was not happy with this and thought the appropriate thing to do was get everyone out. "Come on!" he continued, looking frustratedly at those around him. "Come on! Come on! Everyone out!" he shouted, waving our attended guests in the direction of the open door. "Off you trot."

Complying with his manic command, but slightly bemused at the urgency of it, everyone went slowly out of the door. All non-fire service persons were now outside milling together, looking lost. He made his way to the doors where he now instructed them: "That will have to be it for today, thank you for coming, any questions please don't hesitate to get in touch," and on that note he came in, closing the door behind him. We all looked at each other.

"Ok get this lot cleared up and get that bloody telly outside in the bin!" came his final command.

And that was that we thought. Later that shift the telephone went, the designated watch room person answering, followed shortly by a request over the station tannoy: "Telephone call, sub, it's Reuters on the phone for you." Somebody who was in attendance had obviously thought the whole debacle and irony of a fire safety video actually becoming an incident in itself was newsworthy, and had contacted Reuters News Agency.

After a brief explanation of what had occurred, the Subo thought no more of it. But no, the next day The Sun newspaper covered it as well as it being a news item on Radio 1. The next day wasn't to be a pipe and slippers day. We paid the price for his embarrassment in extra drill.

28

The end of the course was closely getting nearer. Final exam week was about to be here. This would be a day of written exams, covering just about everything we had learnt, followed by a day of drill sessions. This would be various pump drills, ladder drills with both ladders we used at the time (105 Ajax ladder – wooden with two sections and the three section Lacon metal ladder). After weeks of practice and preparation, we were told both exams and practicals had to be passed at 80% and above, or we wouldn't be able to pass out and could be back squadded. So, no pressure then?

The day arrived for the exams. I had spent my spare time in the evenings revising, as had my colleagues. I had spent my weekend at home with the family trying to have a couple of days not thinking about the fire service. As I may have mentioned previously, the subject matters were many and varied. Endless lists, properties of this etc, etc.

Preparation done; the exams went relatively well. Even though it felt like being back at school taking my A levels. This time there was more pressure, my future career depended on me passing them. I can't remember what I got, but can remember feeling well relieved that I had passed.

29

The day of drills came. Lots of running around barking out clear commands and looking extra enthusiastic. Part-way through the day with officers armed with clipboards wandering around attentively writing and ticking things off, occasionally picking a firefighter and sending them inside. After a short time, they would return to the drill square head down looking really pissed off. You could see members of their squad eagerly asking what was going on. I was to find out myself shortly exactly what was going on.

We had just finished a series of drills, when the barking order came in my direction. "Firefighter Cooke fall out and follow me" came the voice from one of the officers armed with his clipboard in hand. My heart immediately sank. Following him off the parade ground, we went into a room. A couple of other officers were standing around and looked at us when we came in, but didn't respond in any way.

"OK, firefighter Cooke, we've been watching you on various ladder drills and to be honest you're not up to standard," he informed me.

I just stood there looking puzzled. In my mind I thought everything was going fine, nothing had gone wrong. I had given extra enthusiasm. Barked out instructions nice and clearly.

"We're going to need to see more commitment, Cooke, if you're going to pass your ladder drills," he continued.

I stood there not really knowing how to respond to him. "Yes, sub," I responded to him, downcast.

"At the end of the day you'll have to do several of the ladder drills again," he continued. "This time make sure everything is done by the book, lots of enthusiasm," he said with a look of concern on his face now. "If you fail, Cooke, you do know you're at risk of being back-squadded?" he concluded.

I nodded.

"Right, back to your squad," he said, pointing at the door as if I had lost my way. Feeling dejected, off I went, wondering what I had done wrong. I was going over the previous drills in my mind as I jogged back to my squad. I couldn't think of anything I had done. These were team drills – what had I done?

Arriving back at my squad just as a break was called, we all jogged back in again to the engine house for tea and biscuits. Stood there, tea in hand, the other members of my squad then questioned me as to what had happened.

"Apparently, my ladder drills were not up to scratch and I'm going to have to do several of them again at the end of the session," I informed them.

They looked as puzzled as I did.

"Fire service bullshit!" my friend Phil quickly interjected. "You didn't do anything wrong, none of us did," Phil continued. "They're playing mind games again, putting the pressure on to see how you react." Looking at me, he said, "Don't give them the bloody pleasure, just go do it again. I'm sure more will be pulled aside," he added with a hint of contempt in his voice. Sage advice as always.

So, I did, completing the drills in exactly the same fashion as before, this time to be greeted at the end with a "Well done, lads, no problems there, off you go" from the new instructor watching. Clearly Phil in his wisdom was right. Another opportunity to put us under pressure.

Exams now passed, we were getting that step closer to the end. The short colder days of winter were slowly edging now into that lovely time of year, early spring. This particular day though, winter was not for letting its grip go. The perfect opportunity, the instructors thought, for an exercise that was to throw everything at us.

All sat at our desks – in came one of the instructors. The usual stand to attention was as always adhered to. "Sit down," he said. All seated, we gave him our full attention.

"Ok, everyone, something a bit different," he continued. "Today's exercise: we are going to rescue several casualties that are trapped in a sewer system," he informed us with a sly grin on his face. We knew exactly the one he meant. The one we had used on many occasions for different scenarios and the very one used on our first wearing of breathing apparatus. Pointing now to the white board, he quickly sketched a plan of the system and what appliances he wanted to be connected, to provide water, as the drill was going to be wet.

"The scenario is," he continued, "an unknown number of casualties have been reported trapped at the end of the system and need rescuing," pointing to the sketch he had just completed. "Two problems though: one, there seems to be a blockage, so the system is filling with water; and secondly, there are also unknown chemicals involved, so rescuers are going to have to wear breathing apparatus and chemical protection suits," he said, clearly not able to hide his glee at the prospect.

So we could all experience the delights of this, we were split down in our squads so that one squad could do the pump operating and BA entry control and help with the dressing and undressing of the CP suits. To my delight, my squad was chosen to go first in CP suits for the rescue.

You may have seen the type of suits I'm describing on the TV. Bright yellow with a clear plastic panel in the front for vision, gloves and boots built in. Fire kit was worn but without your boots and wet legs. Getting into these suits was a performance in itself. Definitely a two-person job, if not three persons.

We were to go in, in teams of two, following the sewer pipe until we reached the casualties and then exit hopefully with casualty in hand. The first couple of teams started up their BA sets and pulling the top half of their suits over their heads by their dressers, they were then zipped up and ready to go. The sewer system was set up as you'd find it in real life. Metal removable lids into a square chamber with metal foot plates cemented into the wall, allowing you to climb in and out. At the bottom this gave access to a four-foot circular concrete tube. More access points were along the route. As the pipes were running downhill these became slowly deeper and deeper. Water was being pumped by hose into the top access point. What we weren't told was the far end had been dammed and the only way to get the casualties out was to bring them back out the same route you went in.

My BA partner and me were now fully donned and ready to hand in our tallies to entry control and get started. We had handheld radios on our BA sets, but the problem was that to operate them and transmit you had to pull your arm out of the sleeve of the chemical suit to press the transmit button, then get your arm back in so you could continue. We climbed down into the shaft, visibility really poor because of the cold. Once your breath was exhaled from your BA set, it went into the CP suit and immediately condensed on the see-through visor, which just made everything a grey blur. This meant again pulling your arm out of your sleeve to try and wipe the condensation away. You can imagine the effectiveness of this if you've tried to clear a car windscreen on a frosty morning. The other problem with these suits was because they were designed to keep the outside air out, they did the opposite and kept your exhaled air in. To get rid of this you had to repeatedly bend and squash the suit so it exhaled, farting air through a one way valve every so often with quite humorous consequences. You can imagine none of this was designed for purpose.

At the bottom I shouted up to my partner that it was clear to come down. This was yet another problem: everything sound wise was now double muffled. To get audible sound you had to literally shout everything. On top of this, freezing cold water was showering down on top of me. Down on all fours I crawled into the pipe and waited for my colleague to get down, and hearing him shout that he was ok off we both crawled.

Sloshing our way down the pipe the visibility, on top of the condensation, became darker. We reached the bottom of another manhole. This being square-shaped gave more space. The lid had been partly opened so as to let in a bit of light.

Down the next pipe we could hear the sounds of the other teams in front of us. Shouting in between the breathing noise of the BA sets. They sounded as though they were working really hard. The water was slowly freezing our hands and legs from the knees down. Reaching the base of another manhole, I cleared my visor and heard over the radio a message from one of the teams that casualties had been found and they were exiting with one. I crawled into the next section of pipe and immediately I could hear and see some movement in the pipe.

"I think there is a team coming out, let's wait here so they can pass," I said, or should I say, shouted at my partner.

We took the short time to try and clear some more visibility and fart our suits. Whilst we did this, I could feel the water was getting deeper. It was now sloshing well above my wrists and knees and feeling colder.

The other team reached us, breathing heavily; one crawling backwards, dragging the casualty, or should I say dummy; the other attempting to push against the flow of water.

"Outgoing team," shouted the heavily breathing rescuer.

We moved to the side and as they passed tried to assist with the movement of the dummy. The sound of us all breathing in this chamber was really loud.

Once they passed, we continued along, the water getting deeper and my hands and lower legs starting to go numb. We could hear more noisy commotion as we crawled further along. Then I met the feet of the other team now on their way out with a dummy. "Outgoing team!" I could hear him now also shouting. I could also see that with all his exertion and heavy breathing his suit had blown up to look like a large yellow 'Mr Blobby'. I thought we can't pass in this tube – we'll have to crawl backwards to the last manhole base where there's room to pass. Shouting at my colleague to crawl back, off we went. The suit of the person coming backwards was so blown up he was now acting as a dam thus making his progress even harder. We let them pass, then our radio went, "Team Alpha three, can you give me a gauge check, over," came the voice of entry control. Because we both had to pull our arms out of our sleeves to check our gauges and use the radio, it meant that we couldn't answer immediately.

"Team Alpha three, can you give me a gauge check, over?" came the repeated request.

We both checked our gauges, my colleague passing his verbally to me and then I passed them to entry control over the radio; entry control, happy that we had enough air, ordered us to continue.

The water was now a third of the way up the sides of the pipe, and I was getting colder and number. Reaching the third manhole shaft which was slightly larger than the others, we could see but not very clearly because the lid at the top had been opened but only enough to let some light in. Here was where the exit had been dammed, and the water was now a couple of feet deep. The dummies, or should I say casualties, left there now partly submerged.

The dummies used by the fire service remain the same, full size made from thick canvas, filled with sand. This meant head, legs and arms all flexed about like a fully unresponsive casualty would do. The adult ones were made to weigh about twelve stone. The only problem was canvas allowed water to be absorbed and when wet sand becomes considerably heavier. These dummies were soaked through.

"Just grab one and let's get out of here," I said to my partner, "I'm bloody freezing."

"I know, I can't feel my legs!" he shouted back at me.

The dummies had a loop at what would be the back of their head, but considering they didn't have faces it could be the front. The water was rapidly getting deeper and all I wanted to do was get out, so I grabbed the dummy by its loop and dragged it behind me. No proper casualty handling here, and to be perfectly honest the dummy was now being dragged under water.

We got to the previous manhole area where complete chaos ensued. Two teams were trying to advance in but had met the previous team exiting with dummy in hand. None could pass in the sewer pipe. For some reason the exiting team had come back down the pipe towards us. The water now was halfway up the sides of the pipe and still rising.

"Check your air," shouted my partner to me.

Pulling my hand in, I reached my gauge and put it to my BA mask so I could read the luminous dials. I had 100 bar, and my colleague had 110 bar. The trouble was that we were working harder now, dragging this soaked dummy under water. We really needed to be out before our low pressure warning whistles went off at 55 bar.

While we waited and had more space, we squeezed our now inflated suits. Not farting now but making bubbles under water. The radio was going mad with entry control wanting updates from teams and warning of low air. The teams were so busy the task of answering the radio now becoming secondary to getting out.

Making room, the team in front came into the square chamber suits so blown up they looked like they were going to pop. As they squeezed out of the pipe a sudden rush of built-up water that their suits had been damming behind them suddenly rushed into where we were. There was an instant shock of icy cold water rushing past us. The chamber then filled with chaotic shouting teams, trying to communicate with each other. One team had followed behind the pair with the dummy. The other had stayed at the manhole further up.

My partner and I stood up, left the dummy on the floor to make room. We were doing things the wrong way round. Instead of outgoing teams taking priority, the incoming team was taking priority. This was now becoming what you could call "A cluster @x".

Somehow, with loads of shouting and squeezing, the incoming team went past and crawled through into the next section of tunnel which was now over halfway full of water. The other team set off into the tunnel to make their exit. My partner and I knelt back on all fours, now half-submerged in cold water. I felt around in the water for the dummy's strap and off we followed.

I was getting really cold even though we were working hard dragging this deadweight. There was certainly no buoyancy in the thing. All our suits were blowing up with exhaled air and it was now getting near impossible to get rid of it. The water felt like it was passing over our neck and shoulders. Then the sound of a low air warning whistle went off. It sounded really loud in the confined space. It was coming from the team ahead. The entry control was now going frantic over the radio and progress seemed to come to a halt again.

We were getting very close to ours going off and I thought it's not going to be long before we are underwater. A sudden shaft of light appeared from the top of the manhole cover and a voice shouted down: "Alpha two, is that your whistle going off?"

At that moment a second whistle went off.

"Yes!" came the now slightly frantic shout back.

"Get out this way and leave the casualty there" came the order from above.

We went back to give them room, but the water was now level with our heads and this was not a good feeling. We watched as they climbed up one at a time, whistles sounding. When the first one got near to the top, I could see four hands stretch down and grab the suit pulling him out with a sharp yank. Not a very dignified move. His partner followed suit.

A voice came from above. "How are you for air?"

"Ok, I think, but we are getting close," I shouted back.

"Right, quickly make your way out through the sewer," he replied.

The other team that was with us in the chamber decided the water was now too deep and they were not for going any further. "You get yourselves out," one shouted. "We'll follow after you."

I was determined we were going to get this dummy out, although if it had been a real casualty they would have long since drowned.

We now had to duck down to get in the pipe which was nearly to the top with icy water. Because our suits were filling with air, our buoyancy pushed us up to the top of the pipe. We were, for a short time, divers. Not what any of this gear was designed for. This was hard work and for a short period even though we were in a pipe, it became slightly disorientating.

"You ok?" I shouted at my teammate. I couldn't hear any response, just the sound of water. I was starting to get to the point of panic, thinking I was not going to drown but suffocate in a big plastic suit. Then there was a sudden release of water, and you could physically feel the water level drop. Somebody must have released the dam at the bottom, giving us instant release. Then at that point my low-level warning whistle went off. All we could do was to continue our exit and hope we had enough air to get out. We got to the first manhole and again a voice from above shouted down: "Leave the casualty there and get out". Up we climbed into visible light, frozen, with extremities numb and desperate to get out of these suits.

We were guided to the dressing area where we were unzipped and helped out. BA still on, I was sucking on metal at this point and pulled my mask straight off. A position you should never be in.

This was an exercise destined to fail. It was maybe an opportunity for a bit of a beasting, but really it was to reinforce the point we had been taught many times. That was, pardon the pun, don't get tunnel vision. You can be so focused on the task in hand, you forget the bigger picture; that is when disaster can strike. The other team that had gone forward had to be rescued. That's when the decision to release the water was made. The team that we met had made the right decision. The situation had rapidly changed and was no longer safe for them to continue. They allowed us to get out with the casualty we had and made their escape. Though if the water had not been released, a question mark also hung over them.

The exercise was repeated later, allowing those who had not worn in the sewers their chance to shine. The result was almost exactly the same. Lessons to be learnt and never forgotten.

31

One thing that all firefighters, emergency workers and I have in common is that of humour. Humour is a great release. It would become one of the most important and enjoyable parts of the job. Whether it was the banter around the mess table or practical jokes which were almost compulsory in the early parts of my career. Sadly, less so as crews got smaller and the fear of offence now a modern-day plague.

The sight of a firefighter going to the toilet and whilst sat there pleasantly contemplating the world, suddenly finding a plate of flour shoved under the toilet cubicle door, followed by a massive blast of air from a BA cylinder. The result once trousers pulled up, would be the emergence of a flour covered upper body and trousers in flour lines. Exiting from the toilet to a tumultuous roar and cheer from the gathered spectators. Just one example of the type of japes that would not occur today.

The ability to find humour in a situation and to be able to laugh at oneself without offence I think was one of the attributes of being a firefighter. It was one of the things that I started to learn on this initial training course. We were being put under stress and pressure, but we laughed together as a team and now as friends.

32

I can remember attending an RTC in which three young men not wearing seat belts had lost control, rolling their car several times. One casualty was thrown from the vehicle lying in the middle of the road, a second had been thrown out but had ended up back underneath the vehicle which was now astride the wall that ran along the side of the road. The third casualty had remained in the vehicle.

Myself and the other casualty care instructor crawled under the vehicle to attend and medically assess his situation. My colleague who really should have gone by the name 'Windy' lay on his tummy. A third colleague crawled under behind him to see if he needed anything. At that point Windy gave out the loudest, longest fart you've ever heard right in the direction of the person trying to give assistance. "Cheers for that" came the response from the poor recipient and although this had been done in his fire kit, it soon filtered through into the confined space.

"What the hell have you been eating?" he continued, gagging.

Then I got a lung full and joined in gagging. All I could see was his now big grinning face. The casualty thankfully with face mask on now, and with his own private oxygen supply, was still unresponsive and unaware of what was going on around him.

You could do nothing but laugh at the absurdity of the situation, and we did when sat back in the mess room.

Humour would also be used regularly when dealing with people, especially when people are frightened, stressed and anxious about their situation or other loved ones around them. A little pun or quip could lighten the situation.

"Am I going to be ok?" could be the question.

"Yes, yes, absolutely fine, we've only ever had problems with people on Wednesdays" could be the reply, that day obviously being a Wednesday. People usually found the irony in the response amusing. Silly little responses along with a smile or held hand could work great medicine.

But what was said also had to be carefully monitored. In casualty care one thing you are taught is that hearing is the last sense you lose. Even an unresponsive casualty may still be hearing what is going on and said around them. A bit like talking to someone who is in a coma. That voice may be the first thing that they hear and respond to.

This would be evident at another RTC where two people were trapped in their seats after a head-on collision. Both had been collared to immobilise them and both were being administered oxygen via masks. The extrication was taking some time. One casualty was unresponsive but breathing normally, the other was conscious but dazed. With the collars on, both were looking straight forward with their heads being held from behind, each by a firefighter. One casualty had emptied a cylinder and was onto their next. Sam, one of the firefighters holding the unresponsive casualty's head, was asked if anyone needed anything. Sam pointed his gaze to the floor where the empty cylinder was lying. "You can take this one, it's dead," he said, meaning the cylinder was empty, but there was an immediate distressed panic response from the semi-conscious casualty.

"No, please God no please, please no" came the now crying casualty.

Sam realising his enormous gaff started apologising profusely. "No, no, she's doing fine, I meant the oxygen cylinder was empty," Sam said in panicked remorse.

Others around her quickly trying to reassure her all was ok.

Not funny at the time but hilarious back at the mess room.

There are some situations where humour can neither be found and nor is it appropriate in any way.

I remember back to that interview with the three officers and one of Mr Nasty Officer's questions was: "And how would you deal with the serious injury or death of a child?" I remember sitting there and thinking for a moment, having just become a father with a young child myself at that time. "I really don't know" came my honest reply. To be truthful, I didn't, and up until that point it wasn't something I had even thought about and certainly not how I would respond or deal with it.

"I really don't know, it's not something I have had to deal with," I repeated.

"But there's a very good chance it will be," he quickly interjected.

I quickly ran the question again in my mind.

"I would hope that the training I'm given would be able to enable me to do the right thing in that situation, but to say it wouldn't upset me or affect me in any way then I'd be lying."

He nodded and moved on to the next question.

This brings me to a situation where I and more importantly one of my new colleagues would be confronted with.

34

The shift started as normal with parade. There we were all lined up at the rear of the engine house. Why the rear, as at most stations they nearly always paraded at the front of the engine house. Stood behind our fire kit, neatly on the floor in front of us. The Station Officer and Subo stood clipboard in hand facing us. The Station Officer looked at the clock on the wall and as soon as it got to 9.00am, he gave the order, "Parade shun." Then turning his head towards the then lined up off going watch and continued, "Off going watch dismissed." At which an eager off going crew made their exit. He then went through who was doing what, at which point when the firefighter's name was called a quick "Sir" was given in response. This was an event happening all around the country. Firefighters being given their position on each vehicle, either in the front if they were driving that shift or if they were in charge. Or in the back wearing BA. That shift I was to be number five on the water ladder.

Today though there was a new face in the line-up, a new probationer had arrived fresh from training school. We all knew that feeling he must have been going through stood there, nerves mixed with excitement. The Station Officer gave him a warm welcome and he was allotted a place in the back of the water tender or second pump as we also referred to it. "Parade for your duties fall out" came the order to dismiss and after coming to attention and turning to our right, off we trotted to our vehicles to start all our equipment checks.

Probationers for their first few tours of duty at this station were put on the second pump. This was the one that would turn out if there were smaller incidents that only needed one pump but would also go out with the first pump to larger incidents. This gave them more hands-on experience. The morning went as normal checks finished followed by a quick pot of tea. Then an hour's physical training. Tea and toast then out for drill until lunchtime. They gave us a good drill session so the new probationer had a good run around. Then a quick shower and dressed ready for lunch. The lunch was duly interrupted part way through when the bells went down. Off we all ran, the Gaffer picking up the turnout sheet en route.

"Flat fire," shouted the boss, giving a pull off copy to the two drivers so they could see where we were going. The flat was above a shop on the way out of town. We wove our way through the busy daytime traffic, turned a corner where the traffic had now slowed right down to a crawl. There above the shop smoke and the lick of flames were billowing out of a first-floor window. The usual line up of people stood around, pointing at the window as though a group of very short sighted and unobservant firefighters were just arriving.

"Access is around the back," said the boss. "After the zebra crossing," he instructed.

"Access is round the back" came the repeat message over the hand-held radio from the second pump. Just to confirm the situation.

We drove past and turned up the next turning, I am sure to the dismay and confusion of those pointing at the obvious. Blind idiots they must have thought. A small unmade street was at the rear with a now large accumulation of people who were looking very distressed. A lady was on her knees surrounded by people who equally looked anguished, trying to console her. Not a good sign.

We jumped off the pump to be met with the distressing sounds and shrill screams of the woman clearly in distress. People immediately started shouting at us. "There's a child in there" came the voices in unison. "Her little girl is still in there," they informed us.

The driver had already got the pump into gear and had run to the back to open the tank and revved the engine to get the pressure up ready for the hose reels to be run off. The BA wearers had already started up. The Gaffer quickly turned to me. "Make it persons!" he said.

Turning on my heels, I ran back to the front of the pump and clambered in, pressing the radio's 'priority' button. This sent an immediate message to control which alerted them to override everything and respond immediately. "Call sign go ahead with your priority" came the voice straight away.

"Call sign from Station Officer at this address, this is now persons reported, over." This would immediately initiate the response to three engines and a Senior Officer. Police and the Ambulance Service would also be alerted to attend.

As in the first stages of any serious incident, the scene was chaotic. I immediately got off the pump and started hauling hose reel, dragging it down the backstreet so that there was plenty for the two teams of two BA wearers to pull in behind them. My next thought was to start setting up a casualty care station. Running back to the pump and grabbing the trauma care pack and defibrillator, then laying a sheet down, I got everything set up and ready to use. Oxygen, burnshield, airways and knowing what type of casualty we would be dealing with paediatric airways and bag valve and mask. The second driver was already wheeling the positive pressure fan toward the door. I grabbed it with him and helped set it up ready to go by the back door. This was now ready for when the BA crews asked for it to go on. Sirens could be heard in the distance getting closer.

The mother of the missing child was now being held in the arms of the Gaffer clearly and understandably severely distressed. The third pump had arrived, their crew quickly making their way to see what they were to do. Our Gaffer beckoned over to one of the firefighters who wasn't wearing BA to come over. He handed the mum into his care, allowing him to get on with his job in hand. He immediately got onto the hand-held radio to get an update from the crews inside.

One crew with a hose reel had gone up to the first floor into the bedroom, kitchen and living areas to locate and knock the fire down. Outside was a flat roof that was on the same level as the first floor. This was also nearly level with the street. I grabbed another reel from the second pump and dragged it 30 foot down the street from the pump and threw it onto the roof. Clambering up, I made my way to a window. At the same time the third pump had got into a nearby hydrant and grabbed a ladder to go back around to the window which was on the main road above the shop.

"Can you see if I can vent through this window?" I shouted through the chaos to the pump operator who was also acting as entry control.

The pump operator went over the radio to the BA teams asking if we could vent. The reply came back yes but don't put the fans on yet. Pulling my visor down on my helmet, I swung the hose reel branch into the corner of the window. Great cracks appeared and with another blow it shattered. Thick, black, hot, toxic smoke billowed out, forcing me to crouch down to allow its escape over my head. I reached up to smash the bits of glass that were still hanging in the window frame. It was just hot smoke that I could see in this room – there was no visible fire or glow coming through it. The scene outside remained frantic, hectic and still distressing.

More spectators had come to see what was going on, and a group had gathered around the distressed mother. I fired several sprays into the room, which was still issuing smoke quite badly, to try and cool it down. Ambulances and police were now in attendance, the police removing as many unnecessary people away from the scene. The paramedics were getting ready now for what they may be confronted with.

Maybe only a few minutes had passed since our first arrival but from the outside it seemed like ages. A jet had been run around to the shop side of the fire, and a ladder had been thrown up to the window. Flames had broken through this window and the jet was now firing water into the room. In the frantic early stages of rescue, time was of the essence. Only crucial messages were transmitted from crews. This meant that those in charge were blind as to what was going on inside. This added its own stresses to those already in place. The order for the fans to go on came from the crews inside – this meant they must have got control of the fire. Two fans had been set up ready. One in the doorway and the other covering the whole of the doorway with its jet of air. The fans started up and the noise was deafening, but the effect almost instantaneous. Smoke billowed out of the window and any exit it could find. Within a couple of minutes, I could see the floor of the room I was looking in, the black smoke had now changed to grey and was a mixture of smoke and steam. I reached over the windowsill and had a good look around the room just in case. When I did this, I could hear the sound of the crews breathing heavily and the muffled shouts of them communicating to each other. Thinking that when they found the casualty it would be quicker to pass the child to me through the window and I could quickly pass the child to the waiting paramedics. I was about to shout in when came the message from one of the BA crews to the officer in charge over the radio. "This is team alpha one to entry control, this is now a Foxtrot One, repeat Foxtrot One over" came the breathless voice. This was sadly code for a fatality. But what was unusual was that there was no crew exiting with child in hand. This was not a good sign; a crew would nearly always bring a casualty out so that all attempts could be made for resuscitation.

The room was now clear of smoke, and I could see through onto the landing area. As soon as that message had been passed, I could see the Gaffer and Sub enter into the building and a few moments later onto the landing towards where the crews still were.

I climbed in through the window and placed the hose reel branch on the floor just in case it was needed and followed them onto the landing. The smoke had all vented now and everything was just a blackened mess.

Then there was the image that confronted me. The two crews were stood in the bedroom, with the face of the firefighter with the jet on the ladder also looking in, face deadpan. The two gaffers all looking at what was left of a bed in the corner of the room. On the bed, or should I say what was left of the bed as only the springs of the mattress remained, was the badly charred little body hunched over head down, bottom in the air. Obviously well beyond the state where resuscitation could even be attempted. The BA wearers continued standing there, their breathing now slowly getting back to some state of normality. The looks on our faces said it all. I think we were all there taking the image in as a permanent photograph, forever to be logged in our minds.

"Ok, lads, well done, you did your best," said a forlorn boss. "How much air have you got?" he continued. The two crews quickly looked at their gauges, both were ok. "Right, just wait a few minutes before you come out, make sure everything is out and remember this is now a crime scene, so don't disturb anything," he said, turning around, looking at the Sub stood next to him.

"I need to go see the mother, shit," he said, walking off.

I just stood there for a moment looking at the scene and thinking that I was so glad not to be the boss right now. As I said, everything was blackened except for glove prints on the walls that the BA teams had left behind them. Post-fire this was a common sight. The crews whilst feeling their way around the room would pat and sweep their hands along the walls to feel and follow their way around, this left a record in the soot of their movements. This was clearly the seat of the fire where most fire damage had occurred, but had then spread from the opened door up into the attic. One last look at our poor little casualty, I also turned and left the room.

Then it hit me that our new recruit was one of those wearing BA in the room. This was not only his first day on shift as a firefighter – thrown in at the deep end was an understatement. The stress of first shift to be followed by a serious fire, but not only a fire. One with a fire death and the worst of all fire deaths, that of a child. I will not dwell on the scene further; I don't think that I need to. Such a tragedy.

Our new recruit had won his spurs so to speak! But would be left as we all would be, with images that would stay logged in his mind and memory for the rest of his and our lives.

This illustrates that when 'the bells go down' at whatever time of the day, at that moment firefighters the world over have no idea what they may be going to attend and what they may be called on to do, or experience. That's why the adrenaline rush never diminished.

35

The light was now clearly visible at the end of the tunnel. Just another week until passing out parade for the whole course, then an extra week for those in our brigade. During the past few weeks one of the extras to the course with it being residential, had been the nighttime exercises off station. A couple of these had been arranged at larger fire stations that had the facilities to hold them. Fully kitted up, off we would go in our fire engines as a convoy to where the exercise would be held. Driving through the streets in our vehicles gave us the first taste of being firefighters, although no blue lights and sirens. When we arrived, various scenarios had been set up and the whole thing would be treated as an ongoing incident, including messages to and from Control, this giving it a little bit more feeling of reality.

Some off-station exercises would be held in derelict or empty buildings or on industrial sites. This would become part and parcel of the life of a firefighter. Our Brigade was, and still remains, very keen on regular holdings of many different types of exercise across many locations. Smaller incidents would be set up with several surrounding stations that were close together. Larger ones with stations brought together from around the brigade. Large fires were simulated with lots of casualties.

Chemical incidents, road traffic collisions with various types of vehicles involved, even train and aircraft incidents. Training, training, training was our Brigade's Mantra.

36

In that same spirit of preparation, it was our time now to practise everything for our pass out day. Marching had, after 11 weeks, become second nature, no more "Spotty dog" marchers. We would march around firstly in full fire kit in front of the gathered crowd. Proudly accompanied by the Brigade's very own band. A quick inspection, then a series of drills would be carried out. All in front of the gathered dignitaries, friends and family. Pump drills would be set up with several jets pointed from around the tower, firing water into the window on a floor. Then on the sound of a whistle they would move simultaneously into a floor higher up and whistle sounding again would all move back down. An oil fire would be lit and a group of firefighters' jet spray in hand would move forward and extinguish the fire. The smoke house would stand in as a house fire. BA wearers entering in to put out the fire and ladders put up to rescue a casualty at a first-floor window. For some reason the casualty was dressed as a clown. One of the workers at the training school would dress up at each pass out. A tradition for which I haven't a clue.

This and lots of other things were planned for the big day. We obviously were very keen for everything to run smoothly and look good. Then at the very end a change into our full undress uniform for a final march around onto the parade square for our last inspection. This time no fluff or hairs or any imperfections would be pointed out to us. Just the odd question and a congratulatory handshake from the commandant and accompanying dignitaries.

At that point we didn't have a clue which station we would be posted to after passing out. Rumours were going around that we would know very soon.

Phil and a couple of others from my squad thought that it would be a great jape to pretend that they had seen a list pinned on the wall in the training school instructors' office.

"Mark, we've seen the list of where we are going to be posted," Phil said, confronting me head-on.

The others keenly were standing behind him. Informing me where he and a couple of the others were going, pleased as punch. He then informed me of where the list said I would be going. I knew when I joined that we had to agree that we would go anywhere in the County. But the place he named was the furthest town away from where I lived. It was at least an hour's drive away; my face said it all. "You're having me on?" I replied.

"No, no, it's definitely there" Phil came back.

This was the worst possible news I could hear. It was the last place I wanted to go to and the practicalities of it would be a nightmare. They could see my reaction but kept up the pretence.

After all the excitement of passing exams and now practising for our big day. I felt punch drunk. I even rang my wife at home on the payphone expressing my disappointment and anxiety.

Phil later, after discovering my stress at this news, quickly relented and informed me of the truth.

"You Bastard'" was my quick response.

"You take things far too seriously" he came back.

He was not wrong. That jape finished with, I could now get back to enjoying the situation. But the question did remain, where was I going to end up?

The day arrived when I was to find out. We were each called into the commandant's office one by one. There he sat with the list in hand. "Sit down, firefighter Cooke," he ordered. "Have you enjoyed the course?"

"Yes, sir," I quickly replied.

"You'll remember these days for the rest of your life," he continued.

I nodded.

"Have you any preferences as to where you might end up?" he questioned me.

"No, not really," I lied, considering what had just recently gone on with Phil.

"You're going to somewhere I have actually served at myself," he continued, telling me which one it was. The station was the very one that I had visited, with that youth group months before.

"That's great," I quickly interjected. My thoughts quickly remembering that visit and the fact that little did I know at the time that I would end up serving there at that very place.

"It's location in the brigade will give you a good variety of incidents in your probation," he explained. "It's known for when it gets something, it is usually dramatic. Some of the best jobs I've been to were there," he informed me.

"Thank you, sir, I'm sure I'll enjoy it there," I ended.

Then on the way out, the realisation. It was a station with a turntable ladder! The turntable ladder played a big part in firefighting in the early years of my career until the decimation and extreme cutbacks that came after the 2002 national firefighters' strike.

That's another story, maybe for another time.

37

One incident again in the early hours of the morning on a cold winter's night. The bells went down, the printer churning out the call details.

"Persons Reported!" came the shout. "It's up the high street," he continued.

Off we quickly drove. The high street consisted of three-storey Victorian buildings with shops on the ground floor, covered with a glass canopy over the pavement. Above the shops were flats whose access was from the rear. As we drove to the incident, we could see the rear of the buildings all the way up the street. Smoke was rising from one area three quarters of the way up. The smoke was coming from the far side, the shop street side. There was nothing visible from our view, so we proceeded on the main road to the front of the shops.

Because this glass canopy protruded out over the pavement, the turntable ladder was put on the pre-determined attendance to gain access to the flats above. It was thought that the large ladder didn't have enough reach. For some reason the turntable ladder wasn't on the initial turnout. The crew on the turntable ladder, hearing persons reported, had been to find out details of the call when they realised which part of the main street it was. They immediately contacted control on the red 'bat phone' to inform them that they should be in attendance. This obviously cost time, and they were delayed.

As we drove up the street and got nearer, we could see the top half of a male body, hanging out of the window, all bent over the windowsill, smoke issuing over and above him.

"We're going to need to get the ladder up to him quickly," our OIC said. Turning to the driver he said, "Get onto control and make sure the TL attends."

"What the..?" came his next response and as we all looked we could see what had caught his attention.

The canopy was made up of two-foot sections of glass panels reaching out from the building out to the edge of the pavement. The panels held in metal frames a Victorian glass canopy. One panel had clearly shattered, spraying glass all around the pavement underneath. What was alarming to see was from this point underneath the canopy a large trail of blood led off and across the street. We all obviously visually followed it as the pump came to a halt. The blood trail went up the street about 50 yards to a telephone box on the junction of the street. There half in the phone box and half on the pavement was another male, naked, now surrounded by a pool of his own blood.

The boss quickly grabbed his hand-held radio. "Second pump, get someone with a first aid kit across to the guy in the phone box," he ordered.

We all scrambled out of the cab to get to the rear of the pump to dismount the ladder from the pump's roof. This was a four-person job. Whilst we were doing this, I could hear the boss shouting up to the man hanging from the second-floor window.

"Stay where you are, we're getting a ladder up to you." His shout rang out above the pump's revving engines.

The man was clearly distressed and breathing heavily.

The ladder now off the pump, we quickly under run it to get it in the vertical position stabilised by the two movable side poles. This allowed two people to pull on the rope to extend the three sections. Up it clanked to its full height about 45 feet. Because of the glass canopy, the heel or bottom of the ladder was further out than the third of its working height position that we always adhered to. At this point we had no idea whether it was going to reach the poor chap when we allowed the ladders' head into the building.

"Head in" came the command from the firefighter in the ladders' number one position. The head went in, just reaching the guy at the window and just touching the glass canopy. A textbook ladder pitch that was thought not doable hence the turntable ladder's recommended attendance. If only training school could have seen that one.

"Stay where you are," the boss shouted up. "We're coming up to get you down!"

A firefighter quickly scrambled up the ladder and guided the chap out and slowly walked him down arms wrapped around him in case he collapsed.

The BA crews quickly got themselves ready to climb up the ladder after he made his way down, to make their way into the building and start firefighting. I ran off the hose reel from the pump, looping it as neatly as I could at speed in loops ready for the guys to take up with them.

Still footing the ladder, I stepped to one side, allowing the first BA wearer with the hose reel looped around his left shoulder to climb up. As soon as he reached the second section of the ladder his teammate followed. I watched as they both climbed; the smoke now getting visibly worse issuing from the window. In they climbed, dragging the hose in behind them.

I looked around to survey the scene surrounding me. In the distance across the road by the telephone box I could see several people attending to the gentleman on the ground. His legs being held high in the air, dressings and bandages being wrapped around one of his thighs.

The turntable ladder had now arrived and had started to set up in the middle of the road ready to get its ladder up.

Police and Ambulance had also now arrived on the scene.

A second BA crew had started up; they also had hose reel in hand and made their way up and into the building.

A third pump from a neighbouring station had arrived also. The OIC directed them to go around to the rear of the building and try and make entry. This they did and quickly over the hand-held radios came the message: "Station officer, the fire has broken through the floor below and flames are issuing through the first-floor window! We're going to try and get a large jet to work."

"Roger that," the OIC quickly responded. This was bad news as both BA crews were on the floor above the fire now. All things were quickly coming together to what could quickly become a disastrous situation. "BA crews, be aware the fire is underneath you on the floor below" came the firm instruction from the OIC.

What we had no idea of was that on the outside simultaneously two things were about to happen. Firstly, the BA crews had made their way to the far side of the room to a closed door. This door was to open onto the top of the stairs which led down to the floor below. The floor where the seat of the fire was. The crew at the back had just got a large jet ready to go into the window and were also about to break down the door on the ground floor to make entry into the flat.

The turntable ladder had now been extended to an adjacent window to the one being used by the BA crews to make their entry. The BA crew, feeling the door, knew that there was a fire beyond and had got themselves and the other crew in the room ready to fire water sprays through. The technique used was to open the door enough to allow several sprays of water into the room. This repeated several times would hopefully cool the hot gases down and eventually allow entry.

This incident happened in the early days of my career before extensive training and understanding of things like 'flashovers' and 'backdraughts' that would later come into effect.

The crew opened the door, but this happened at the same time as the crews at the rear opened the ground floor door and fired their jet into the window. The instant effect was to create a sudden influx of unburnt flammable gases now with its own supply of oxygen up into the room the BA crews were in. This explosive reaction slammed open the door with such force and threw the two BA wearers by the door across the room.

Outside, the sudden explosive noise and force blew the window out where the turntable ladder had just reached, spraying glass down over all of us underneath. A large orange jet of flames thrust itself horizontally out of the window, lighting up the whole scene as though daylight had come. The OIC instantly shouted on the hand-held radios, "All crews get out now", his voice sounding panicked.

Whistles were grabbed and the repeated blasts rang out in the air. This was the call to get everyone out now. Inside the crews didn't need telling. The room's temperature had obviously gone instantly up into the extremes. Temperatures of 1000 degrees are possible in these situations.

I stood footing the ladder, looking up and almost instantly a figure appeared at the window, scrambling manically at the top of the ladder to make his escape. As soon as he was on the ladder, another figure appeared to make his escape. This was not dignified but frantic, firefighters making their escape. At the same time at the other window that had just blown, a figure flew headfirst looking like Superman. He leapt headfirst, grabbing the top of the turntable ladder and was now head facing down the ladder towards the floor. If the ladder had not been there at the right point and angle, he would surely have fallen straight to his death. A fourth figure immediately followed now on top of the upside-down firefighter. Now out of the building they assisted each other into a position to continue their escape. They climbed down, the sounds of their breathing resounding heavily all around. They made their way down and as they got to the bottom of the ladder where I was, I questioned each one of them. "Are you ok?"

Each of them were visibly shaken up and pulled their BA masks off as they got to the ground. The OIC and others had gathered to see if they were ok. This was before the issue of flash hoods, so ears, lower head and neck had no protection, and two had clearly suffered burns. "Get yourselves over to the ambulance," he ordered them.

The firefighter on the turntable ladder was now the right way up, making his way slowly down with his colleague. When the room had flashed over, all four firefighters had been thrown onto their backs. They had fired their hose reels above them to try and protect themselves. What had happened though was with the sudden extreme heat, the water had instantly turned into super-hot steam. It was this steam that had caused the burns to their unprotected areas. Both would have to be taken to hospital. Thankfully it wouldn't be too long before the adoption of Flash Hoods would be taken up by our Brigade.

Post-incident I think the realisation hit our Station Officer that he could have very easily lost three or four of his firefighters under his command. Not through any negligence of his command, but simply by the convergence of unfortunate circumstances.

For several months after this incident, you could hear him discussing the situation with any and every officer who visited the station. He only had a couple of years left before his retirement, and shortly after made the decision to finish his career in Fire Safety. In the time he was to command us, he was one of life's true gentlemen and nobody thought any less of him on the news of his move.

Regarding the two gentlemen rescued, both thankfully recovered. The man found with severe wounds by the telephone box had bravely attempted to climb out of the window and down using the television wire. This had snapped and he fell through the glass, breaking both of his ankles and slicing a large wound in his leg. There was not a telephone in flat and this was in the days before mobile phones. If he had not made his way to alert the emergency services, the outlook would clearly have been very different. A very brave person indeed and an example of how we humans can respond to extreme circumstances and situations.

38

Earlier I recounted that one of the first large fires I attended was to a mill fire. This ended with a very near miss that could have been a tragedy. I was to attend many mill fires throughout my career, all around the County. Just prior to my retirement I was to attend one of the largest and most spectacular mill fires the country has seen in recent years. This mill was in the nearby city very near to its centre, built about 160 years ago at the height of the mill age. It was one of the largest ever built. Several storeys high, a millstone grit building, dark and imposing. It's structure and great chimney stack dominating the streets of terrace houses surrounding it. As well as this main imposing part of the building, attached to it were acres of north light roofed buildings. The north light roofs were designed to allow as much light for the workers inside but shielding them from the direct light from the sun. This was so that they didn't cook in the summer heat.

The mill had not been used for its original purpose for many years with the demise of the woollen industry years before. It was a building, however, not only known to those who lived in the city but also around the world. Particularly in Pakistan, India and Bangladesh. The reason was that hundreds of people from these countries had travelled here to work in this mill and had set up communities around it. The mill becoming known to those families left back in their home countries. Many arrived to live here and work was at its height in the fifties and sixties. Although now its looms and textile machinery had long since been removed, for the space to be predominantly used now for storage. Many of the mill fires I had previously attended had usually progressed rather rapidly. Today this was to be slightly different.

It was mid to late morning and as a crew we were out and about our own town in our appliance, merrily carrying out our duties for the day. Over the radio we heard an assistance message asking for more pumps to attend. This was followed shortly thereafter by an informative message updating control of the situation. At this point it was a fire in the basement, location unknown but with smoke issuing. Shortly after this came a message to our appliance to move down the valley to go standby at a station nearer to the city where the mill fire was. Off we set and as we travelled a further assistance message came over the radio with a larger number of appliances now being asked for. Our radio went again with control now asking for us to go now to the city centre station where the mill was, to go standby and provide fire cover for the town. Driving nearer, we could see a plume of smoke rising; this was light and wispy. Then, as we approached a large road intersection, across our path the sound of sirens and then a fire appliance racing, its lights ablaze. Soon after more sirens, this time the colour racing across us was bright yellow. Three vehicles from Yorkshire Ambulance Service H.A.R.T. The Hazardous Area Response Team. These in recent years had become a familiar sight at any large fire or serious incident. Their role in this situation was to provide back-up medically, not specifically for the public but for the fire crews. If any crews got into a situation where they needed medical attention they were immediately on hand.

Over the radio came our call sign again. We were now being redirected again, this time to the fire itself. Control gave us instructions to proceed to the rendezvous point. At any large incident a rendezvous point would be set up and a control vehicle would be sited usually nearby. When so many different vehicles were now attending this incident, what you didn't want is a traffic jam surrounding the scene. Now with our blues and twos going, we started dressing into our fire kit and made our way there. We arrived a few minutes later behind several pumps that were parked along the side of the road within a couple of hundred yards of one side of the mill. Smoke was issuing at street level but there were no visible flames. Our OIC picked up the crew tally from the dashboard in front of him, street level but there were still no visible flames. "OK, you know the drill, just wait here."

He got off the pump and made has way to find the control vehicle. In our brigade we had at that time a state-of-the-art vehicle with lots of communication facilities, TV screens, map boards etc so that the senior officers in charge of the incident could find out who was where and doing what. Or where they wanted things deployed. Certain crews from particular stations were trained and assigned to operate and work in the control vehicle. Our OIC would make his way to this vehicle and hand in our crew tally. This had our vehicle call sign and the names of all the crew on that vehicle. This meant there was a record of everyone there and what they were doing. We sat in our vehicle awaiting our OIC's' return. We all maintained our attention on what was developing in front of us. Smoke was still issuing from windows at street level, billowing in clouds across the road. An increasing group of firefighters with BA sets on their backs were setting up ready to be dispatched into the building from this side.

Then walking towards us appeared our OIC. "Right, gents, everyone grab a set and a spare cylinder," he said through the open cab window. Then opening the cab door and standing on the step in, he added, "We're going around to the rear of the mill to sector three."

We each grabbed a set and a cylinder out of the side lockers, gathered in a huddle and off we went following the boss. At any incident sectorisation would be put into operation. This basically was if you looked at a building or area of operation the front would be sector one, going in a clockwise direction the next side would be sector two, the next three, and then four. This was to break the fireground up so that it could be controlled more easily. We walked down the road past the usual sound of engines revving, red hoses snaking across the ground from hydrants to pumps and then disappearing into a doorway. We followed more around the building, the place now a hive of firefighting activity, yellow and white helmets everywhere. The white ones usually in clusters, more in busy conversation and gesticulation than physical hard work. Walking past the tallest part of the mill, a stone wall five storeys high, each floor full of tall windows. You could imagine what people's thoughts of this building would have been over 150 years ago when it arose from the ground. The whole city from all around able to see its statement of power and industry. Impressive and imposing just two words to describe it. There in front of us we could see a gathering of fire engines again with the usual sight of snaking red hoses on the ground. Nearby firefighters stood or sat down on the ground with their breathing apparatus sets on their backs or laid tidily on the floor around. Two breathing apparatus entry boards had been set up each with two operators. One with a handheld radio, the other writing information down on the board.

"I'll go to the sector commander and find out what he wants us to do," our OIC informed us and off he went.

We stood about, looking to see what was happening around us. There was an open entrance large enough for lorries to enter, hoses going in and disappearing into the darkness. A short time later we could see our OIC returning to us.

"We are to stand by as BA crews and wait until we are needed," our OIC informed us.

Crews came in and out over the next 20 or 30 minutes. Going in fresh and then exiting hot, sweaty and sometimes dirty with blackened helmets.

Our time came and I was to be number two in a three-person team. The BA control designating our team's call sign and the task to be followed. Ours was to follow one of the hose lines into the doorway on the left; this apparently led down into the basement and the team that were already down there had been tasked to reach the fire front and attack with a large jet.

"According to the last update, the team that are in now hadn't got to fire yet," the entry control officer informed us. "They're going to be getting near to the point of needing to get out before their whistle time," he continued. "Everyone happy?" he concluded, looking to see our response.

We all replied or nodded and then started up and finished dressing. Making sure each other's gear etc was ok and flash hoods, gloves etc covered our skin. Radios were tested and we each handed in our tallies to the BA controller checking us over again and then checked our gauge readings matched what was written on our tallies. He did this so he could work out each of our whistle times and when we should be out of the building. This completed, off we went.

Entering the doorway, a large stone stairway met us going down. We followed our designated hose in clear visibility – this meant our progress was quick. Once at the bottom of the stairs we could see the basement open up before us. I say open up, about 20 feet in front of us, we were confronted from floor to ceiling with a wall of cardboard packing cases. To the left was a six-foot gap between the packing cases and a stone wall running away from us on the edge of the basement. Only very light wispy smoke could be seen at the top of the room, and we could see the hose we were to follow went down this gap. Off we went in our three-person conga. Maybe 20 or 30 feet further on, the light began to fade and we were surrounded by darkness, and we became reliant on sound and touch. Each of us following the hose now held in our hands. The sound of voices and heavy breathing came next. The other team we were to replace obviously making their exit. I could hear the voice of one person updating the situation to the person in front of me, our team leader. "We've nearly reached where we could feel the fire" came his now slightly laboured voice. "But we haven't been able to put any water on it yet," he continued.

"Right Ho," our guy responded, and we stood still for a moment to allow them to go past us. Carrying on, we could feel the heat getting stronger, causing us to lower our stance, closer to the floor. Then the sound of crackling and the odd bang could be heard. The hose had now obviously been dragged to a point where it was in loops on the floor ready to be pulled further in. This held us up for a moment as we found out where it went. It continued following the gap between the wall and packing boxes.

"I've found the branch," our leader informed us. He picked it up and we also got into position behind him. BA control came over the radio and asked us to take a gauge check. We complied and had plenty to carry on. "Let's see if we can get closer" came our leader's next instruction. There still wasn't any visible sign of the fire as we continued and then an orange glow appeared through the smoke. Opening the branch, we all felt the sudden jolt of the hose as our jet of water sped off into the inky blackness in search of the appearing then disappearing orange glow. This jet reaction made each of us behind our leader grab harder and lean into the back of him to keep him steady. The fire continued to crack and bang and then came a sudden blast of hot steam like a wave.

"Think we've started to hit it," I said to each of my colleagues.

"Yes," they both responded.

We moved the jet around in front of us, causing more hisses, and crackles and bangs. The orange glow disappeared, then re-appeared in a different place. We chased it around for a while and when we hit it a blast of steam followed.

"We had better take a gauge check," I pointed out.

After each looking at our gauges, we all came to the same conclusion. It was time to make our way out, so shutting down our branch we began to retrace our steps. When we got to the bottom of the stairs it was still clear visibility. A white helmet met us, not wearing BA. "How far in before the smoke is too thick?" came his question.

"About 20 feet then you have to crouch to get clear air," my mate responded.

"Can you wait here for just two minutes?" he asked. "I just need to check something out–" pointing over to the right side of the basement where the packing cases were and continued off into the distance.

"Ok," we replied.

Off he sped, following the packing cases down and out of our sight. We just stood there and waited. Two or three minutes passed; we took the time to check our gauges again. Thankfully none of us were near to our whistle time. But the problem now was the teams in the other sectors must have made some headway with their firefighting and consequently they had started to push the smoke in our direction. What was clear and visible now was beginning not to be.

"We're going to have to make this persons in a minute if he doesn't return," I said to the other two.

The smoke now started to edge nearer. If you have seen the Only Fools and Horses special where Del and Rodney are dressed as Batman and Robin and reappear running down the street through the fog, this was the scene that met us. Out of the smoke jogged the white helmet coughing and when he reached us in clearer air bent over, clasped his knees with his hands and sucked in great lungfuls of air.

After a few seconds he tilted his head upwards and looked at us. "Bloody hell that was close," he exclaimed. "Cheers for staying."

"We nearly declared it persons reported," I replied.

"Yes, one minute it was clear then I could feel and see it coming at me," he explained. "I started running, thankfully there was only one way I could come back, and it was a straight line."

"Ok, let's get out of here before it gets any worse," our team leader declared.

Climbing up the stone stairway he told us that he had gone to check if there was a link from this part of the building to the next. He had found you couldn't get to it from the clear side of the building to this side. He said that he had found a lift shaft that was worrying. Out in the open air, we made our way to entry control, shut our sets down and debriefed entry control as to what we had done. He told us to go and service our sets and standby as there was a good chance we would be going back in soon.

At this point there were 25 pumps in attendance and 125 firefighters with them. As well as Yorkshire Ambulances, 'Hazardous Area Response Team' and numerous police controlling the crowds coming to see what was going on. Because of the smoke that was drifting and getting ever thicker, properties nearby were being evacuated and their occupants sent to a close by community centre. More teams were being committed from all sides of the building into the basement. It was looking good that this magnificent building would be saved. Shortly the time came, and we were told to go to entry control again as a three-person team. On arrival, although it was the same entry control operators, we were going to be put on another entry control board, as after each one was filled and used it remained as a record and a new one started. Again, we were tasked to follow the same hose line and continue firefighting. We reached the entrance and stone stairway; the difference this time was smoke was now up to the stairway. On entering, it soon became impossible to see. We followed the wall and the hose as we now knew the lay of the land. Again, we met an exiting team and they said that they had found a sliding door on the wall that gave better access to the fire. They then explained that they had pulled the hose and branch back and we would find it looped on the floor with the door shut. We carried on our little conga until we reached the looped hose on the floor. This time I was at the front of the team as team leader. On we went past where we had been previously. The teams before us had done a great job at pushing the fire back. Reaching around in the darkness, I found the branch and picked it up.

"Let's find this door," I instructed to the other two; we all patted our hands, feeling along the wall, searching.

"Got it" came the reply. This was a big heavy door on big metal runners that slid along the wall. "I've found the edge but I'm not sure which way it slides," he said.

"I'll get ready with the branch," I replied. "We're better off crouching down."

Although it was pretty hot where we were, the thought came to me that we had been fighting the fire earlier on this side of the wall, so there must be another way to where we were now that the fire had gained access previously. The problem now was it could build again; this time if we advanced too far and it did that, we would cut off our exit.

"We need to keep an eye on what is going on behind us if we go through this door," I said to my teammates. Or more of a listen and feel the reality in that blackness. This was an example of not knowing what the layout was and how rapidly the situation could change and lead to tragedy. We couldn't feel any heat in the door, but we had no idea what was behind and although the previous team had advanced through, the fire could also have advanced as well.

"I'll just see if it will move and in which direction," said my teammate. The other got behind me and I could feel his hands on my back and shoulder.

"It's coming back towards me," he updated. "Tell me when you're ready."

"Ok, now," I replied.

He slid the door slowly a few inches at a time so we could see beyond. We couldn't. It was total blackness, but there was no glow or visible flames. What there was, was a blast of heat like we were opening an oven door. I blasted the darkness with the jet for a few seconds. But nothing came back at us.

"Let's move forward," I said.

In we moved, crouched, it was definitely getting hotter and once we got into this next room, after a short time we could see flashes through the smoke ahead of us at ceiling height. This was always a sign to be very careful and aware of. 'Dancing Angels' they were known as. I opened the branch up and directed it at the ceiling, moving it from left to right and back again. A couple of years previously we had received updated electronic BA Boards now linked directly to our ADSU (Automatic Distress Signal Units) on our Breathing Apparatus sets. If we were in distress, we could press a red button on them, this would send a signal telling entry control exactly who was in distress. It worked the other way as well: if in an emergency they wanted an immediate evacuation, they could set our ADSUs off. There were three ways of knowing an emergency evacuation was instigated. As I have just mentioned for those wearing BA, handheld radio messages could also be used. One old-fashioned but very effective way was the repeated blasts on a whistle. A whistle that every firefighter carried in their pocket.

Then it came over our hand-held radio, the repeated message: "All teams evacuate from the building now; I repeat all teams evacuate now!" At that point our ADSUs started sounding. Repeated squeals sounding on each of us. I shut the branch down, put it on the floor and turned to my teammates and shouted over the sound of the ADSUs, "let's get out of here now". We turned, grabbed each other by one hand on the back of our BA sets, this time number three leading and me at the back. Through the door we had so carefully gone through, to the wall. We knew all we had to do was to follow the wall and it would lead us straight back to the stairs. This meant that our escape was speedy, but very noisy with the sound of the radio and our ADSUs.

Reaching the stone stairs we were greeted by another sound; the repeated blasts of a whistle being directed down the stairway. Whoever was blasting at the whistle must have heard the sound of us coming up. "Come on, hurry up, get out now" came his frantic instructions. Nearing the top, I could see daylight and the chap with the whistle. Just as I made my way through the doorway a sheet of flames shot right over the top of us, coming from left to right. Startled, we crouched and then ran as fast as we could. Making our escape from this sudden hot breathing dragon. BA teams were exiting now frantically making their way to a safe area. The dragon breathing hot fiery flames from its mouth, the open garage type door which was clear when we had gone in. Officers were running around, encouraging teams to get clear. Other teams were now outside firing their hoses at this beast. There was a queue at each entry control of firefighters wanting to be shut down. Many like me breathing very heavily after our sudden inflicted exertion. We were met by entry control officers desperate to make sure everyone on their boards were now safely out. Tallies quickly checked and marked off the board. The fire we had been battling on all fronts in difficult circumstances had, as it so often does, finds and searches for the three things it needs to survive: heat, fuel and oxygen. It was apparent now that it had found a way through from the basement to the ground floor and once there had found the one thing it was desperate for – oxygen. It now had it in abundance and made the most of it. Rapidly expanding and advancing in all directions that it could. This had been seen by those in charge outside, hence the rapid evacuation. In hindsight a very timely call indeed. It was a miracle that no firefighter had been trapped, injured or at worst had been killed.

Most of the hose lines apart from a few in our sector were into the basement, left in the hurry and were now redundant. Frantic effort went into shutting them down and the running out of new hose in replacement to now fight the fire from the ground floor and outside. The battle continued. What happened in the next half hour was one of the largest and most rapid accelerations of a fire most of us had ever seen. The fire as I have mentioned searches like a living organism for its needs. It had found a way into the tallest and largest parts of the Mill. Whether through an open door, stairway or lift shaft, it wasn't bothered, just feed me and let me get ever bigger. Despite all the efforts, and at one point the thought that we had beaten it – but no, it had come back and thoroughly exerted its authority, sadly now at the expense of this magnificent building. We and the rest of the city watched as the massive plumes of smoke and raging flames rose high into the sky. It was a sinking feeling, like the fire was just letting us know, I am the mighty one here, not you with your puny efforts to stop me. TV footage went on to national television and news coverage around the world. Particularly those countries where so many had come from to work there.

The end of an era.

39

The day finally came, yes, it was pass out day. Last minute preparations, things to set up for the day ahead. Everyone was filled with excitement and pride. Pride in finishing three months of what was filled with both the best of times and some times that would not be forgotten. But we had learnt the importance of teamwork and that the fire service could not operate properly and efficiently without it. No situation in the fire service, whether it is a house fire, road traffic collision or chemical incident is ever resolved individually, it's dealt with as a team effort. Each person playing their part with reliance on each other. There we were, exhibition drills prepared. Seating stands for dignitaries, officers, and families all set up. Appliances and equipment washed and polished. Everywhere tidied up and cleaned, ready for people to arrive. We were dressed in our finest, uniforms neatly ironed, shoes bulled up to gleaming. All stood around, Sellotape in hand patting each other, removing dust and hairs. We looked like a group of well-dressed monkeys grooming each other.

It was time for our guests to arrive and we made our way outside to meet and greet. My wife had arrived with our young daughter in hand with my mum and dad. I gave my wife and daughter a hug and a kiss, then kissed my mum, then stood there in my uniform in front of my dad to receive his strong handshake and a greeting of "Well done, lad, you look very smart!". This meant a great deal to me. My Dad had served in the REME in the war, landing on the Normandy beaches and making his way through Europe. He served in Europe until his demobilisation in 1947. He was a Londoner who was sent up to Yorkshire as part of his training. When after being on fire watch at the local mechanics institute where a dance was being held downstairs in the main hall, he met my mum, and they married in 1945.

He was serving in Europe where he met a fellow soldier who invited him with a group of other soldiers and officers to a group of Christians who met for Bible studies and discussions. After some time, I remember him telling me he knelt with this friend on the barrack room floor, prayed and dedicated his life to Christ and became a Christian. After his time in the Army, he started his early life with his then young family in farming. But this was not what he felt called to do. So, he started studying Theology and became a Minister of Religion. This led to my mum and dad living in various places around the country.

Some of you good at maths may be thinking well how old does that make me. After my older brother Barry arrived in 1947 and my sister Yvonne in 1949, my other brother Paul arrived in 1953. I was an afterthought, not arriving until 1962, at which point my father was 40 and my mum 38. I was born in Luton, Bedfordshire. When I was two weeks old my dad moved to Leeds in 'God's own county' to Pastor a church there. I was so close to being a Yorkshireman born as well as bred. He continued to pastor churches around the country until at the point when I was six years old, they moved back to Yorkshire to live permanently in a village near to the town where I was soon to become a firefighter. My dad continued to preach at churches all around Yorkshire and beyond, right up to shortly before his death at the grand age of 98. My mum passing shortly before, aged 96.

When I was to get on station and fellow colleagues found out that my dad was a Londoner, and I was born in Luton, some thought it was fun at times to label me as a "Cockney". Any discussion regarding the South, "Oh ask him" would come the retort. "He'll know, he's part Cockney." All I can say is those 'Bow bells' must chime a bloody long way!

My dad was ever the encourager in life. If I had said to him "and I want to become a pilot", he would have replied "great, go for it" in an ever-positive manner. The day I had passed all my entrance tests and had my interview, I called in to my mum and dad's house on my way home. At this point I had not mentioned to anyone that I had been applying to join. So, it was news to them when I called in, fully suited, and they asked what I had been up to. "Well, I've just been for my final interview, and I've been accepted into the fire service," I told them. There was an initial stunned silence and pause before my dad responded. "You do know it can be a very dangerous job, don't you?" he came back. "Yes," I replied.

Again silence, then the return of Dad's enthusiasm, followed by a story of how he had seen the London Fire Brigade in the Blitz, racing down the road, bells ringing out with all the firemen hanging onto the side of the fire engine. "I think it's moved on a bit since then, Dad," I said sarcastically.

But as I said, his congratulations meant a lot.

The day went well. It was now early spring, and the weather was fine. We proudly marched around onto the parade ground in our firefighting kit, ready to carry out our practised drills in front of the expectant crowd. Racing around in our fire engines, lights and sirens blazing, proudly showing off some of the things we had learnt during our time there. Then a final march around, now dressed in our finest, band playing and to the cheers of the onlooking crowd.

Food was provided in the mess room, the bar was opened, and chat and mingling took place between recruits, officers and family.

Whilst the invited had been waiting for us to get ready for our display, I found out afterwards from my dad some of the things that had been said to them by, I think, the Chief Fire Officer. He had said to them that they should be very proud of us for what we had achieved in getting to this day. He said that most, if not all, will have been pushed to our limits, both physically and mentally. That we were about to embark on what he considered was the best career in the world.

My parents left, taking our daughter home to babysit her, so that my wife could stay to enjoy the evening celebrations.

40

We all now knew where we were going, those in our brigade spread all over it. We had one extra week to do then we would go our separate ways. But we had built up friendships that still last to this day. United in that bond of being on the 120th Brigade course. We had all struggled and succeeded together.

You may remember right back on that first day of the course a young lady sat ready to start with us. Sadly because of different circumstances she wasn't able to pass out with us and was back squadded to the next course. I am happy to say that when the next course completed, she passed out to become the Brigade's first whole-time female firefighter. What is amazing is that as I write this, notification has just come from a post on the Brigade's retired social media group of her retirement. After well over 30 years of service she has hung up her boots. That is retired not died. Well done and what a coincidence.

The last day. We all said our goodbyes to one another. I know this all sounds very sentimental, but everything written about here was also intermingled with humour and an awful lot of taking the piss out of each other. No failure, shortcoming or defect was ever allowed to go unnoticed, or be reminded of. In today's world and I am not going to use the word constantly being banded around now, could be considered as bullying and harassment in the workplace. At times when I look back it was very rare when it may have overstepped the mark. It certainly was different times then. Have we gone too far in the other direction today? I would say a resounding "yes". When people lose their careers because of a comment on social media that does not fit in with certain thinking, I think that is a dangerous form of fascism. The generation of my parents fought a war for the freedom of expression and thought. My dad would say that part of the cost of that is hearing things at times clearly you would not agree with and may be offended by. There is no place for any form of bullying or harassment at work, but in the cause to irradicate this it does seem at times that in doing so it has also gone on to destroy innocent fun in fear of offence. I remember the days when an OIC would call into the office, door closed, those who may have had a dispute or falling out. Get them to resolve the issue, ask them if they were happy and get them to shake hands. Then an instruction of "that is the end of it".

So as my children keep reminding me speaks the dinosaur.

41

When we were given our posting, we were also advised to find out when our watch was on duty and before our official start, pop into the station and introduce ourselves. I called in one evening and nervously introduced myself. I was taken then into an office to meet my new Station Officer. Even though I was in my civilian clothes, I stood to attention in front of him.

"Nice to meet you, sir, my name is Mark Cooke," I introduced myself.

"Ok, calm down, lad you're not at training school now" he came back in response. "How are you at running?" he continued.

"Yes, fine," I replied.

"Good," he said. "We run here each shift, all weathers," he said, looking at me straight in the face. I suspect to see my response.

"Great," I said quickly back at him.

"How's your volleyball?" he then questioned.

"To be honest I've never played," I replied.

"You'll learn quickly, we take it very seriously here," he continued. "You've got your probation to get through so keep your nose clean and your head in your books, I expect all of my probationers to do well, it reflects on me."

"Yes, sir," I responded.

"Right, lad. I'll get the sub to introduce you to the watch," he said and with that our meeting was over.

The sub came and took me to the mess room where the lads were sat down having a pot of tea. At that time there was 15 on each watch, 12 on duty, three on leave each tour of duty. Which was two day shifts, starting 9.00am until 18.00 hours, followed by two nightshifts from 18.00 hours through to 9.00am the following morning.

There was quite an age range sat around the table. Two or three with grey or greying hair with one or two bars on their shoulders, indicating either Leading Firefighter or Sub Officer. Then the rest with two or three fresh young faces sat down at the opposite end of the long table. These were the others who were at various stages of their probation. One I was to find out was nearly at the end of his. I was to make probationer number four. The probationary period at that time was two years followed by a further two years to become what was classed as a fully qualified firefighter, which meant that at qualified you received full firefighters' pay.

I had been told to take my fire kit with me when I visited the station.

"Have you got your gear with you?" asked one of the subs sat opposite me.

"Yes," I replied.

"Right, I'll find you a spare peg on the rack to put it on," he continued.

We went out to the kit room, found a peg and there I hung my gear next to the rest of the watch's neatly stacked fire kit. Ready for my first shift.

A couple of weeks later, I arrived early at the station ready for my first shift, not knowing really what I was doing. Firefighters were scurrying around, mops and buckets in hand, everyone seemed busy with a job to do. I was later to find out that on a morning everyone was given a job to do. As well as washing the pumps and mopping the engine house floor, we were expected to clean all the toilets, sweep the floors, empty the bins and after breakfast make sure the mess room and kitchen was spick and span and the mess room floor mopped, and tables cleaned.

I went into the mess room feeling like a real spare part. There was a guy with a white coat on over his uniform, wiping tabletops. Seeing me obviously not knowing what to do, he questioned, "First day, lad?"

"Yes," I replied.

"Go get your fire kit, stick it on the floor by the doors behind the pumps," he instructed, "then come back in here and grab a pot of tea, you've got plenty of time before the rest of blue watch arrive."

I dutifully did as he said. Then over the next 15 minutes or so, people started to arrive, coming into the mess room, the off going watch chatting to some of the faces I recognised from my visit. It got to 8.55 and everyone started to make their way to the engine house ready for parade. A neat line of fire kit stacked in a row with some of the guys stood behind, relaxed and chatting away to each other.

"Morning," each one said to me as I approached my fire kit. "Morning," I nervously replied and stood behind my kit.

On the floor facing us was two sets of kit, one with a white helmet on top, the other with a yellow helmet with two stripes on it. Opposite us stood in a line in front of the pumps the off going watch had lined up, ready to be dismissed. Then in came the Station Officer, chatting away with the Station Officer from the off going watch.

Before each parade and change of watch, each officer in charge would do a handover, passing on any relevant information they needed to know. This was also written in a book just in case of a lack of time or opportunity with incidents. He stood behind his kit, facing us. Then on the dot of 9.00am a voice came over the station tannoy. "Parade, off going watch dismissed." And with that instruction, the off going watch came to attention, quickly turned to their right, and then scurried off to get their gear from the appliances.

The line next to me either side came to attention. I quickly followed suit but looking a bit like Corporal Jones from Dad's Army, one step behind. There I stood nervous but also excited, ready to start my career in the Fire Service.

I have only written a snippet in this book, regarding the variety of incidents over my just short of 30 years' service. Most from the very early years. Some of the largest incidents with 20, 30 and on one occasion 40 appliances in attendance. Incidents where the sights were too graphic and distressing.

Incidents involving animals, plus hundreds of routine car fires and rubbish fires too mundane to write about. During my time I was to attend one of the country's major cities riots. Shortly before my retirement I was to attend the largest mill fire in recent history at one of Yorkshire's bigger cities. This was nearly a disaster in which many firefighters had a lucky escape including myself. Again, a story maybe for another time.

One thing that has escalated over time has been the increase in both verbal and physical abuse towards firefighters. I have had both bottles and fireworks thrown at me. This always seemed to increase in the run up to bonfire night. I was also to attend moorland fires that went on for days, many times.

Over that 30-year period the career of a firefighter has changed dramatically. As with all change, some good and some, to put it bluntly, terrible. Budgets sadly have continued to be cut. The station I have just been describing now only has one pumping appliance and the Station Officer, now Watch

Commander, travels in his own vehicle and covers two watches.

One thing that did happen over my time was the use of home fire safety checks, and the fitting of smoke detectors in people's homes. This has dramatically reduced the number of house fires. Because they alert in the early stages of a fire, fire deaths have also fallen greatly. Intervention in schools has also reduced the number of hoax calls and the awareness of the fire service's role in and to the community.

My time in the fire service changed also. As time went on my interest in casualty care progressed. As our training in this area became much more in depth and the introduction of more equipment continued, I became a watch-based Casualty Care Instructor. I attended the very first International Casualty Care First Responder Course. We also received a very up-to-date, at that time, turntable ladder which had a cage that could be attached at the end of the ladder and operated from there. Yes, my favourite piece of fire service equipment and yours truly became a cage operator.

After the 7-7 bombings in London, the government realised that it was not prepared for any terrorist incident involving a dirty bomb. This could be Chemical, Biological, Radiological, Nuclear and Explosives, or CBRNE as it's known. Funding came from central government for the larger Metropolitan Brigades for equipment and vehicles to deal with this. Part of this was the provision of large decontamination units that could be used anywhere in the country and set up to decontaminate large numbers of the public in the event of another terrorist incident. Our station became one of these and training took place every three months on the equipment with a full set up of everything twice a year. This happened with other emergency services and agencies, sometimes with live casualties.

Later we also acquired and were trained on the new wildfire unit. This was a Land Rover with its own water tank, but it also had its own pump and two very high-pressure water lances. The Land Rover towed behind it, what you could describe as a horse box. This was filled with lots of different equipment to fight large area fires, particularly moorland in our county. The Land Rover and trailer were fitted with blue lights and sirens. I became an operator, so I went on an off-roading course and blue light training. An identical trailer arrived, but this was to carry a decontamination unit and equipment specifically to use on firefighters.

43

One of the things I became involved in, in the last few years was the young firefighters' scheme. Our station had its old separate Auxiliary Fire Service building next to it converted into a mini fire station. This had a classroom, small kitchen area, toilet, kit room and an appliance bay, complete with its own mini fire appliance. The fire appliance was kitted out with smaller size and lengths of hose which was more manageable. Plus, on the roof a scaled down ladder.

Courses were held from ages 12 up to 18. They could be six weeks, 12 weeks, up to one and two years. Those aged 16 could take a two-year NVQ.

The abilities of the children varied. Some had struggled at school. Some had behavioural problems and had been excluded from school. These courses were held on our rota days off and as our shifts constantly moved on, an opposing watch would take the course when we were on shift, and vice versa. Each course would have at least two firefighters as instructors and at least one teaching assistant, depending on the difficulty and behaviour of the students.

We had on the wall a chart listing the rules of attending the courses, regarding expected behaviour and discipline. Each young firefighter had to sign this and take it home for their parents or guardians to agree and also sign. Each person was given their own fire kit, which they were expected to look after and after use put neatly on their own pegs.

Discipline we soon found out had bypassed many of these young people. At the start of each session the first thing we always did was hand round a biscuit tin for them all to put their mobile phones into. There was always one who would announce, "I haven't got mine with me today, sir." Only later to be found looking at their hands under the desk.

Some schools we had to ring after a class and pass on any behavioural problems or issues that needed addressing. Each class, if we were doing classroom work, this usually happened at the beginning. We would then announce a "dress for drill" order at which point they were expected to quickly go and get dressed into their fire kit.

For some classes this came quickly, and they responded well to this kind of discipline. Others it took weeks and sadly on a few occasions the odd one or two, it was decided by us and the school, they were asked to discontinue. Classes were attended by both boys and girls and on occasions we would have more girls than boys. We also made the course available to those with physical issues and learning difficulties.

Considering their particular needs to be able to attend, we would start with basic hose running. Then pump operating. They could do this either from a hydrant or an open water supply. A favourite was to travel to a nearby open water supply and do the drills there. As previously mentioned, they had their own ladder. This was a two-section aluminium alloy ladder that was extended with its own rope like the fire service ones. We would put this up to the first floor of the tower and each of them were asked to climb up. They were taught the correct way to do it. To some this was a terrifying thing to do. Some could only go maybe two or three rounds up or would get two thirds up, realise where they were and would freeze. They were encouraged to go further if they could, if not to come back down. Over time, after more attempts and with the encouragement to go a bit further – we would also get those around to also encourage each other – they would achieve reaching the top. Again, they were taught the correct way of getting off the ladder and into the window. To see the faces of those who had struggled and then overcome their fears to achieve this, then receive applause and cheers from their fellow comrades, was very rewarding.

Another favourite on the course was when they wore breathing apparatus. They had their own sets on their pump, each with a cylinder and mask to wear. The only difference was that they were a lot lighter to wear and the masks were not connected to the cylinder – they breathed the air through the mask.

The next station to us had its own "Smoke House". This was a building with a crawl at the bottom and then the setup of a house and attics with roof beams and an exit in the roof with a bridge that went across to the tower. Using this we could do various exercises, crawling around in the dark, clambering over and under various obstacles. Later in the course we would use artificial smoke. The kids loved this. Again, some would have to overcome various fears to achieve their goals. With encouragement from us, their teaching assistants and fellow young firefighters, the sense of achievement for some was great.

For those on the shorter courses, a pass out parade would be held on station where parents and guardians would be invited to attend and watch the young firefighter carry out a drill in front of them. A senior officer would attend, and certificates would be handed out to each one at the end.

Those on the longer courses, particularly those doing an NVQ, their pass out would be held at headquarters on the training school parade square.

The young firefighters' scheme was carried out at several stations around the county. At the pass out parades all the different groups would come together and parade at the very ground I had held mine on many years before. Exhibition drills would be practised on station ready for the day. All would be carried out in front of a grandstand of friends and family, teachers, local dignitaries and senior officers. Everything was done to make it a big event for all who attended.

The engines were lined up, each crewed by the young firefighters and us. The PA system would announce each school to arrive. Then sirens blaring and lights flashing on, we would speed to about the awaiting audience. Young faces beaming with excitement and pride. Carrying out our well-practised display in front of an equally proud and cheering audience. After this, everyone would line up to attention, get back on their vehicles, drive in front of the onlooking audience, hanging out of the vehicle's windows eagerly waving to those there to watch them. A parade would then be held, each standing in lines to attention whilst speeches would be made. Afterwards a buffet would be held and a time for us to mingle and be introduced to attending friends and family. This was an opportunity for us to tell them what they had achieved and overcome. Leading these groups was at times extremely challenging but at others very rewarding.

I remained as a firefighter throughout my time. Promotion never really appealed to me. I liked it in the back fighting fires or providing casualty care as well as being on a watch. There are many other stories I could share, maybe another time? When I hung up my fire boots for the very last time, it was as any firefighter will tell you an emotional time. I have seen many a time firefighters shed a tear or desperately trying to hold them back when that final dismissal comes. The excitement of retirement but also the thought that there would be no more adrenaline-led response to the bells going down.

I went on to work on Ambulances for four years after that. Rewarding in a totally different way. But I can honestly say being a firefighter is the best job in the world!

Printed in Great Britain
by Amazon